THE HAWK ON THE
WESTERN SKY

THE HAWK ON THE WESTERN SKY

*Discovering the Truth
About a Suicide*

JIM BALE

Springbranch Press

First Edition

1. History - Michigan
2. Memoir - J. Bale
3. Psychology - Suicide
4. History - Underground Railroad

ISBN 979-8-218-42143-4

First Printing, 2024

Dedication

For my family, especially my late father, and all families
who are touched by suicide.

I thank Martha, my wife, for her love, support, and patience.

Also by Jim Bale

Pilgrimage to Spring Branch Creek: A trout seeker's journey.
Stories in Stone: An introduction to rock art
Animals of the World: A story for my grandchildren

With Gregg Solms:
A Pocket Full of Puffins

Contents

Prologue: The Lie

"Jimmy, you're first," Mrs. Levin, my third grade teacher, announced shortly after we returned from the morning recess.

The late September day had been windy and unseasonably cold, so no one, least of all the teachers who monitored our recess, complained when the bell rang and called us back into the warm classroom at Three Oaks Elementary School. Today was family history day, and our assignment was to draw our family trees and describe them for our classmates.

Like many of the school's teachers, Mrs. Levin used the alphabet to determine the order in which she called on her students. Mostly, she started with an A, making John Anderson first and me second, but to keep things interesting, she'd occasionally start with a Z. In reality, no one in our class had a last name beginning with X, Y, or Z, so starting at the end of the alphabet always meant that Donna Wolfe, a petite, mischievous redhead, would go first. But today was an A day, and John, I would soon learn, had been excused to stay home and help his family.

The Anderson family owned 160 acres a mile or so south of town near the Indiana border, and apple trees covered most of their land. Each fall, the Andersons harvested their apple crop, and soon thereafter, families from southern Michigan and northern Indiana would converge on their farm to buy crisp red delicious and tart McIntosh apples and fill glass gallon jugs with apple cider. I enjoyed the pie that my mom made with the Macs, especially when she served it ala mode with vanilla ice cream. But most of all, I loved the Anderson's sweet apple cider.

The barn northeast of their farmhouse housed a vintage, cast iron apple grinder and a large, wood press, and with these, the Andersons would make cider from one-half of each year's apple crop. They collected the pressed juice into spotless, stainless steel buckets, which John and his two teenage brothers carefully carried to an enormous 200-gallon oak cask that sat beside their driveway. The harvesting of the apples and the pressing of cider were arduous, time-consuming tasks, so the Anderson family needed everyone at home, even John, the youngest.

Mine was a simple family tree. I only had a brother, and my mom and dad each had only one sister, who both happened to be named Carol. Mom's father, my maternal grandfather, lived alone; his wife of thirty years had passed away from complications of diabetes just before my brother was born in 1953. On Dad's side, there was only his mother, Blanche, my paternal grandmother, and her sister, my great aunt, whom everyone called Aunt Claribel. I began to fidget when my brief presentation ended and my teacher, as well as my classmates, started asking questions.

We spent nearly every Christmas Day, I told the class, with my mother's father in Albion, Michigan, a middle-class, factory town approximately 100 miles west of Detroit. A soft-spoken, slender man with thinning gray hair and a glass eye, my maternal grandfather lived in a simple, one-and-a-half-story house with a galley kitchen, dining room, and living room on the first floor and two small bedrooms upstairs. A tiny downstairs den served as a third bedroom whenever we visited. My brother and I loved our grandfather, especially when he bought us Brach's orange slices at the neighborhood market. But other than picking vegetables in his garden or watching a Detroit Lions football game on the 12-inch, black-and-white RCA television that sat in one corner of his front room, we found little to do in Albion.

Visits to my dad's family, on the other hand, were filled with tractor rides, squirrel hunts, and hikes to the back forty, where we often saw white-tailed deer in the cornfields and woodlots. Dad had grown up on a farm in West Michigan near Paw Paw, a village known for Concord grapes and Charlie Maxwell, "The South Paw from Paw Paw," a skilled utility outfielder who played for the Detroit Tigers in the late 1950s and early 1960s. At the farm, I could walk for hours with my dad or brother, eat grapes right from the vine, and pick sweet dewberries that Mom would make into jam each summer. With luck, I even found arrowheads in the freshly-plowed farm fields.

But I had no grandfather there, only Grandma Bale and Aunt Claribel, who had lived together for as long as I could remember. I looked forward to the visits with my dad's family, I told my teacher and classmates, especially at Thanksgiving, when I could eat my fill of turkey, cranberries, and pumpkin pie. But I had nothing to tell them about Grandfather Bale.

That evening, when I showed Mom my hand-drawn family tree and recounted my painful class presentation, she began to tell me about my grandfather.

"Your grandfather Bale was a tall man, standing all of 6 feet 2 inches," Mom began, "and he loved his son, your dad, and his daughter, your Aunt Carol, just as much as we love you and your brother."

"Like his father and grandfather before him, he farmed the land on which the Bale family had settled after coming to Paw Paw from England more than a hundred years ago. They planted and harvested corn and alfalfa, which they used to feed a small herd of dairy cows, and they raised chickens and pigs. They would later grow Concord grapes and sell their crop each year to the Welch's juice plant in the nearby town of Lawton. Grandfather Bale loved the land, too," Mom said softly, tears beginning to well up in the corners of her eyes.

"The crops, the farm animals, his children, and your grandma were all very important to him."

"One day, while milking cows in the big barn, he heard terrified squeals coming from the pigsty near the pine trees west of the farmhouse. He looked out to see a large hawk swooping down, trying to snatch the young piglets with its sharp talons. So he grabbed his shot-gun, which he kept loaded in the barn, and ran to save the pigs."

"Halfway there, he tripped in the tall grass and fell. The gun went off, and buckshot struck his chest and head. And before anyone from the farmhouse could reach him, Jimmy, he died."

Mom began to cry, and so did I. We sat together sobbing for several minutes, and as her tears subsided, she hugged me again and asked if I had any questions. Choking back tears, I shook my head no.

Mom and I didn't discuss my grandfather Bale's death again for many years, and I never had sufficient courage to ask my father or grandmother about him. What I would discover much later was that Mom's tearful story had been a lie.

This book is the story of my search for the truth. The journey would lead me through a series of family events that ultimately took a pandemic to connect. My search was like assembling a 1000-piece jigsaw puzzle with key pieces missing. It would take my imagination and some guesses to fill the gaps.

At the onset of the pandemic, when isolation became the expecta-tion, I started writing this book on the birch dining room table that we rarely used, or, for that matter, now didn't need, given the new norm of avoiding contact with other people. When it became evident that Martha, my wife, needed space too, I abandoned the dining room and moved to the basement, a place I eventually called the dungeon. Except for the light emanating from the laptop screen and my 25-inch ASUS monitor, the basement was mostly dark and cold, too.

There, I wrote at a mission oak desk that I purchased from an online supplier of Amish furniture. The desk's arrival took nearly five months; the pandemic and the problems with the supply chain seemed to affect the Amish, too. But maybe they had it better, working alone in their wood shops and avoiding us English. The well-crafted desk was worth the wait; on it, my words seemed to flow more smoothly.

I

✦

Ilfracombe

To paraphrase the noted archaeologist Tom Higham, we must know our ancestry to know ourselves. I needed to learn so much more about my family to uncover the truth about my grandfather's death. I wanted to understand our values and traditions and hear the stories passed from generation to generation. Families, much like individuals, are influenced by life's events, and these events determine choices, actions, and consequences. In this process of discovery, I anticipated that I would learn more about myself. And most of all, I hoped that I would finally know how my grandfather died and understand why my family created the lie.

Bale Ancestors, date unknown
Source: Unknown photographer

The Bale story began nearly 200 years ago in Ilfracombe, England, a quaint village that hugs the rugged Atlantic coast in the county of Devonshire. In 1827, Mary Lettaby Bale and William Bale had a baby boy, James, my great-great-grandfather. James, who would live to be 91 and be known in his later years as Grandpa Bale to both family and friends, was the youngest child and the only son of Mary and William. The Bales, on the other hand, had been blessed with six daughters, all older than James:

Susan, Lena, Jane, and Caroline, born in 1814, 1821, 1824, and 1826, and Rose and Lily, whose birthdays fell between Susan and Lena.

Sadly, three of James' sisters, Susan, Caroline, and Lena, would not live beyond their early twenties. Did they die during childbirth, a common occurrence among young Victorian women, or did they succumb to tuberculosis or one of countless other infectious diseases that affected Ilfracombe's inhabitants? Cholera, measles, and whooping cough, diseases we now take for granted, threatened everyone in the Victorian era, and thousands died annually throughout the British Empire.

Or was it something else? Did they contract rheumatic fever, a disorder that damages the heart valves and brings an early death from heart failure, or did they have a fatal genetic disorder that somehow spared James and his more fortunate sisters? I lack answers to these questions and must add them to what will eventually become a long and perplexing list.

James, who likely felt fortunate to be a boy rather than a girl in the 1800s, spent much of his early childhood doing what first-born sons did in Victorian England, following in a father's footsteps to learn his profession. By contrast, his sisters stayed close to home, doing what girls did, emulating their mother and learning how to cook, sew, clean, and bear children.

Just before sunup, James would likely arise with his father and join him in a hearty breakfast of toast with marmalade, a slice or two of bacon, and a fried egg prepared each morning by his mother and sisters. Although freshly-caught fish from the nearby Bristol Channel might occasionally supplement the morning meal, James undoubtedly loved the bacon that his mother bought from the local butcher most of all. The smoky bits of pork wedged between his teeth could linger the entire day.

William, James' father, who had learned the carpenter's trade from his own father, probably demanded much from his only son, even at James' young age. A stern man, William expected that James would observe and reproduce his every action as he used a saw, drill, plane, and mallet to hew, join, and craft wood into doors, cabinets, and banisters. But James had a sharp eye and an eidetic memory, and these served him well as he faithfully copied his father's work.

The sudden death of William Bale in 1834, when James was just seven years old, brought a temporary halt to James' apprenticeship. Although James would later write fondly and, at times, poetically about his youth in Ilfracombe, he never mentioned his father or the circumstances surrounding his death. A terse, handwritten note, a tiny part of our family archives, once referred to William as 'Capt. Bale'. While I believe that this was simply an honorary title given to him by a servant, could William have been a ship's carpenter and lost at sea? Or had he served in the Queen's army, and there is so much more to the story?

William's death, on the other hand, did not surprise me, even though he passed away before the age of 60. At least one-half of all men in Victorian England died before their 50th birthdays, and the plight of women was scarcely better. The death records from the Leeds Cemetery in the northern part of the country tell us that people in Victorian England died from many causes: consumption (tuberculosis); dropsy (heart, liver, or kidney failure); inflammation (infections of various types); and natural decay (old age). Many other deaths, which the record keepers grouped together as 'unknown' causes, resulted from murder, accidents, and suicide. Where, I now wonder, did William and his daughters, Susan, Caroline, and Lena, fit in this long list?

Had it not been for James' older sisters, his father's death would have permanently altered James' life. Sisters dote on younger brothers, nurturing them like surrogate mothers, and James' sisters supported their only brother in the months following William's death. They would help him cope with the sudden loss of his father. A craftsman friend of the family, recognizing the boy's talents, likely took the young James under his wing so that he could continue his apprenticeship. What emerged in James as a result of these events, which we would now call adverse childhood experiences, were self-confidence and resilience. And James gradually became a skilled craftsman like his father.

The grainy black-and-white photograph of their front yard, which has been kept among our family treasures for nearly two centuries, tells me that the Ilfracombe Bales lived comfortably. James and his family had sufficient means to live in a row house, and they likely owned a carriage, a valued possession that suggests they also owned a horse. In their front yard stood a well-manicured hedge, a low stone wall, and a solid wooden gate, features common to many English homes and cottages of the 1800s. To the side was a larger gate, which might enable a horse-drawn carriage to enter the property from the street. Nearby rose the roof tops and chimneys of their neighbor's homes, their abundant smokestacks affirming the reliance of 19th-century England on coal for heating and cooking.

But the photograph says nothing about the things that really matter--the personalities and behaviors of my ancestors and of James himself. Except in tales of fantasy, pictures rarely tell the full story.

Ilfracombe's harbor, date unknown
Source: Unknown photographer

A thin stack of 3 x 4 inch black and white photographs and two pairs of vintage stereographs, which snuggly fit the antique stereopticon I inherited from my grandmother, tell me a bit about Ilfracombe itself. One stereograph shows the harbor at low tide, where numerous skiffs rest on the muddy sea floor. Above a rock seawall, two- and three-story, white-washed, and tile-roofed buildings line the waterfront, and narrow streets extend in orderly rows inland from the harbor. At a doorway stand three men, maybe merchants or sea captains, and two women who may have just exited a shutter-clad building, perhaps a bakery or a fish market. And at the far end of the seawall is the three-story Brittannia Hotel, which beckoned to Ilfracombe's visitors.

Here, amidst the harbor shops, the young James would likely run errands for his mother and sisters. He might visit the butcher shop or the family's favorite bakery, and in between, he might pause beside a pub's open doorway, hoping to hear the sailors' stories as they downed a pint or two of the local ale. Most were the fishermen who caught the herring, pollack, and mackerel that swam in the cold waters near Ilfracombe, but some were sea dogs, men who sailed the stormy waters of the North Atlantic and made the treacherous crossing to the New World. On occasion, James might stand dockside and gaze westward, daydreaming about what lay beyond.

Ilfracombe's location on the Bristol Channel of the Atlantic Ocean drew many to its harbor and beaches. At Hele Bay, Ilfracombe's fine bathing beach, modestly attired bathers swam in the cold Atlantic waters, and afterwards, they might sun themselves on wood and canvas folding chairs that stood in orderly rows on the sandy shore. The rugged cliffs and heather-covered hills rose defiantly from the Atlantic, towering over the beach and its bathers.

Hele Beach, Ilfracombe, date unknown
Source: Unknown photographer

Single-stacked ships frequently steamed into Ilfracombe's small harbor, but most were unsuited for the demands of transatlantic crossings. Rather, their size and configuration suggested that they ferried tourists up the Bristol Channel and past the rugged Devonshire headlands. On warm summer days, the ships' passengers would disembark and gather on the immense wood pier of Ilfracombe's secluded harbor. Then, they might stroll uptown in search of food and lodging. Businesses and rowhouses, built of wood and quarried stone, lined the town's streets and adorned its many hills, which, like those of Hele Bay, rose abruptly from the sea.

People first settled in Ilfracombe during the Iron Age, 2500 years ago, when the Celts of Dumonii constructed a small stone fort, known as Hillborough, on a high point overlooking the harbor. Ilfracombe's fine natural harbor had been formed thousands of years earlier by a granite and mudstone reef that protected the harbor entrance. A century before James' birth, Sir Bourchier Wrey built the sturdy, 900-foot wooden pier to supplement the rock jetty. The snug harbor would become a refuge for ships caught in storms as they sailed the Bristol Bay north to the much larger port of Cardiff, the capital of Wales. Smugglers would sometimes hide their boats in secluded coves not far from Ilfracombe, and they might mingle surreptitiously with other travelers who visited the inns and taverns of the seaside village.

Hillborough Rock, the site of the ancient fort, rises nearly 500 feet above the beaches, and to the west, Lantern Rock, which once sported a lighthouse on its summit, stands 140 feet above the ocean's surface. Near the sea lies Capstone Hill, with its precipitous cliffs and peaks, known to the locals as tors, providing expansive views of the town, the Bristol Channel, and the English coastline. The area's rocky, wind-swept coast beckoned to inhabitants and visitors alike.

I believe that James' thoughts turned often to the broad expanse of ocean that lay beyond the hills of Ilfracombe. A simple pencil sketch of Wildersmouth and Capstone Hill, which James made in his teen years, suggests an affection for the region's rugged landforms as well as a wanderlust that would eventually draw him westward to the New World.

Ilfracombe Headlands
Source: Drawn by James Bale as a teenager

Ilfracombe's population rose steadily during the 19th century, growing from approximately 1,800 people in 1801 to more than 3,600 in the years before James was born. The focal point within its parish, Ilfracombe supported the nearby hamlets of Campscott, Warcombe, and Lincombe, as well as the estates of several wealthy families. Although not as bustling as Cardiff to the north, Ilfracombe served its people well. At the village markets, held each Saturday, local farmers could sell their wares from small, canopied stands, and at the lively stock fairs, held in the spring and fall, herders would display their sheep and cattle.

Three of the town's booksellers opened lending libraries where the young James and his friends could learn about the world. Books like Dickens' *Oliver Twist* and Melville's *Moby-Dick, the Whale*, would grace the shelves. Some books, such as *Moby-Dick*, James might take home, and there he could read by candlelight until he fell fast asleep, dreaming of adventures on the high seas.

During the 1800s, Ilfracombe, some 200 miles southwest of London, became known throughout England as a desirable destination for bathing, as swimming was called at the time. To improve access to Ilfracombe's beaches on Bristol Bay and the hidden coves of Crewkhome, the city's engineers bored tunnels through the craggy cliffs that separated the town from the sea. In the decade before James' birth, Ilfracombe built elaborate community baths near the harbor, and their Doric architecture complemented the natural beauty of the area's coastline. Public baths, the swimming pools of the day, opened throughout Victorian England and on the Continent as people began to appreciate the benefits of frequent bathing.

At the time of James' birth, most people believed that human diseases resulted from bad air, known as miasma. This explanation seemed logical, given that people could smell the stench, or vapors, associated with industrialization, human waste, or decaying animals. That said, some still accepted the antiquated hypothesis that human diseases resulted from an imbalance of the four humors: black bile, yellow bile, blood, and phlegm. During the 1800s, physicians and scientists began to dispel these outmoded concepts. The work of Robert Koch, a German physician and microbiologist; Joseph Lister, a British surgeon; and Louis Pasteur, a French chemist and microbiologist, supported the novel germ theory, which postulated that unseen microorganisms, such as newly discovered bacteria and viruses, caused many human conditions. It followed, then, that good hygiene might mitigate the risk.

Of the three scientists, Koch achieved the greatest acclaim, winning the Nobel Prize in Physiology and Medicine in 1905. His postulates, first published in 1890, remain, to this day, the 'litmus test' for diseases believed to be the result of microorganisms. To accept causality, Koch required that the causative agents must: 1) be found in the diseased animal and not found in healthy animals; 2) be extracted and isolated from the diseased animal and subsequently grown in culture; 3) cause disease when introduced to a healthy experimental animal; and 4) be extracted from the diseased experimental animal and demonstrated to be the same microorganism originally isolated from the first diseased animal.

Like other English towns of the day, Ilfracombe contained numerous churches of the Anglican faith, a far-reaching religious community that now incorporates nearly 40 different faith groups, including the Episcopal Church, which counted the Ilfracombe Bales among its numbers. From the historical records of Van Buren County, Michigan, where James would later settle, I learned that his parents were 'consistent members of the Episcopal Church'. Through church attendance, the young James likely heard biblical stories about love and humility, and these lessons, as well as his deep faith in God, would serve as guideposts throughout his long, productive life. And cherished memories of his Ilfracombe childhood would be the inspiration for the church he would later design and build in Paw Paw, Michigan.

In James' day, the schooling of English boys was typically basic and brief. Although 70% of the men of the mid-1800s could read and write, few could do so with any fluency, and very few were educated at prep schools or universities. Moreover, the education of girls and young women was woefully inadequate; barely 50% of England's women were literate in the mid-1800s. Not until the school reforms of the late 1800s did educational opportunities and literacy rates improve for the people of England.

James received a 'good common-school education' in Devonshire, so said the Van Buren County record, and this suggests that his father's death did not relegate him to a charity school. At a charity school that had been created for orphans and disadvantaged youth, James would have received only the most rudimentary instruction in reading and arithmetic. I found no record that his mother remarried after his father's death, but even if she had turned her attention to a new husband, she nurtured her only son well. James' accomplishments as a builder, architect, and inventor, as well as the books he owned, which included *The American Conflict* by Horace Greeley, the founder and editor of the New York Tribune, confirm that he had a keen intellect and thirst for knowledge that far exceeded the average Ilfracombe schoolboy.

In his early twenties, James began to court Eliza Jane Pugsley, four years his senior. Eliza, the daughter of John and Mary Pugsley, had been born and raised, like James, in Devonshire. I suspect that they met at a supper at Ilfracombe's Episcopal Church, and given their difference in age, it seems likely that they had been introduced to one another by one of James' older sisters.

The conventions of the Victorian Era governed James' and Eliza's courtship; a chaperone monitored their every interaction. They could stroll the village streets together, but they could never touch. James could offer a hand to Eliza only if the street was muddy or if a street crossing posed the threat of a fall or an injury. Not until they announced their intention to marry could they regularly hold hands in public and visit Ilfracombe's shops unchaperoned. Undaunted by the conventions, which we would now consider draconian, James proposed to Eliza, and they married in 1849.

English marriages of the mid-1800s favored men, and until the passage of the Married Property Act in 1882, a woman's assets always passed to the husband on the day of marriage. Did Eliza have a handsome dowry that enticed the young James to propose? And did they use her money to finance their journey to America? Or was she of more modest means, and only their hope for a better future motivated James and Eliza to marry and sail to the New World? Opportunity enticed many to America, not only to find employment in America's bustling eastern cities but also to seek their fortune in the vast western wilderness.

Whatever the reason, James and Eliza declared that they would leave England shortly after the wedding ceremony. The newlyweds' decision to leave England, I believe, reflected the desire and courage to forge their own destiny, much as my wife and I did when we left Michigan after our marriage and moved west to Utah more than 100 years later.

If the young couple had any fears about leaving their homes and family, they never showed. In the summer of 1849, James and Eliza left Ilfracombe on their honeymoon, and at the docks of Liverpool, England, they boarded the paddle ship Unicorn, bound for Ellis Island and New York City. While their life in Ilfracombe had undoubtedly left many enduring memories, the couple would never again set foot in England.

2

⌘

Ships Passing in the Night

The Unicorn, constructed in the Rue End shipyard by Robert Steele and Company, was launched in 1836 from Greenock, Scotland, on the Firth of Clyde. Some 20 miles west of Glasgow, Greenock began, like many seaside settlements, as a fishing village where its fishermen sold and exported the herring they caught in the Irish Sea. As England's colonial empire and transatlantic trade grew, shipbuilding emerged as a prosperous endeavor for many coastal towns, including Greenock, and eventually supplanted fishing as the dominant industry. Today, the Steele's Rue End Street docks, which date from the 1830s, may be Scotland's oldest existing dry docks.

Robert Steele & Company, which succeeded Steele and Carswell Shipbuilders, a company co-owned by Robert Steele Sr., began building ships in 1815. Over time, the name Robert Steele & Company became synonymous with well-designed and meticulously constructed vessels, and upon the senior Steele's death in 1830, Robert Steele & Company, now managed by the next generation of the Steeles, continued to build ships of exceptionally high quality.

Steele & Company designed and constructed sturdy wooden-hulled paddle-steamers, like the Unicorn, for coastal routes between Glasgow and Liverpool or for short open sea voyages to England, Ireland, and the European continent. Later, the small, but sea-worthy ships were re-fitted for the long, demanding transatlantic routes between Liverpool or Glasgow and North America.

The company would also build magnificent clipper ships. At its peak, Steele & Company had launched twenty China tea clippers, a designation for the ships that transported Chinese tea to the waiting merchants in the British Isles. More than a few of the company's ships would win the coveted China Tea Race. This informal but prestigious competition recognized the first ship to make the perilous journey from China to England with a new crop of tea in its hold. According to Mark Howard, an Australian historian, these wood and composite (wood planking on an iron frame) clipper ships, outfitted like exquisite racing yachts, could make the trip from Hong Kong to London in less than 70 days!

Unicorn in Salem Harbor
Fitz Henry Lane (1804-1865), Unicorn, Salem Harbor,
1840 (inv. 600). Fitz Henry Lane Online. Cape Ann
Museum.

The Steele and Company's Unicorn, not to be confused with the British Navy frigate, the HMS Unicorn, sported three masts and a single stack emanating from a reliable Caird & Company two-cylinder steam engine that drove the ship's dual 30-foot paddle wheels at 15 revolutions per minute. Her length and breadth of 162.9 and 23.5 feet pale in comparison with the average 21st-century cruise ship, which exceeds 1000 feet in length.

While I found no information about how the Unicorn received her name, I did learn that tradition, superstition, and some science underlie the christening of ships, a practice that has existed for most of recorded history. At times, the naming of ships seems capricious, left to the whim and fancy of a ship's owner, but in other instances, the naming shows sound judgment. Ship names often commemorate a notable event in the ship owner's life or honor the life of a beloved person, most often a woman. Sailors considered their ships feminine, calling them 'she' or 'her', in the long-held belief that a ship's motherly or goddess-like qualities would protect them.

The Unicorn's bowsprit and billowing white sails might be mistaken, I suppose, for the horn and wings of the mythical creature galloping across the water on foggy Scottish mornings. It seems equally plausible that the Unicorn's name celebrates the ship's unique status as the first vessel in the newly formed British & North American Royal Mail Steam Packet Company of Glasgow, Scotland, owned and operated by Samuel Cunard. In May of 1839, Cunard won a seven-year contract with the British Admiralty to carry mail between Liverpool, Halifax, and Boston. The Unicorn became the first ship to cross the Atlantic Ocean flying the Cunard flag.

James and Eliza, I would learn, splurged on second-class tickets, giving the newlyweds some privacy, a precious commodity in the transatlantic ships of their day. This class provided the young couple with clean quarters outfitted with two stacked bunks, a tiny closet, and a stand with a washbasin. They would share the head, the ship's primitive bathroom, with other first and second cabin passengers, and they would take their daily meals, prepared by the cook and served by the stewards, family style in the Unicorn's galley.

By contrast, the many passengers in steerage had a far more spartan experience. They traveled in relatively unsanitary conditions within the converted cargo hold of the Unicorn and cooked their own food below deck using the meager rations provided by the ship's purser. The steerage passengers slept on straw mattresses in makeshift bunks that held three to six people and often ran two-high along the interior of the hold from fore to aft. Dark, dank, and overcrowded, steerage compartments could seem more like dungeons than accommodations.

Although I could not find specific information about the Unicorn's fares, a second-class ticket from Liverpool to New York on a Cunard Line ship in the mid-1850s would have cost the Bales 20 guineas each, or approximately £21 per ticket. The steerage fare from Liverpool to New York in 1850 cost about £4, corresponding to more than a month's wage for an unskilled laborer. When the Titanic sailed from Southampton, England, decades later, a first-class ticket cost £79 (~$5000 US today), while second- and third-class tickets cost just £13 and £8, respectively.

Even as excited newlyweds who eagerly anticipated their new life together in America, James and Eliza would have found the Atlantic crossing tedious. Twenty or more days confined together with two hundred passengers on the small ship undoubtedly tested everyone's patience and endurance. Unlike those who sail on large cruise ships today, the young couple had no lectures, spas, or nightly shows to occupy their time during the long days at sea. Mostly, their days were filled with the incessant *chug-chug-chug* of the ship's steam engine and the monotonous reverberations of the ship's revolving paddles.

On occasion, a fiddler or a minstrel might entertain the passengers with the songs of the day, such as *Alice Gray* . . . *"Oh, his heart, his heart is broken, for the love of Alice Gray."* Summer squalls might break the voyage's monotony with cooling rains and rolling swells, but the stormy weather could also trigger seasickness in the ship's passengers. Mostly though, the Unicorn's passengers, including James and Eliza, spent their days looking westward, eager to be the first to see the New World.

Among the many ships that made the crossing from Liverpool, England, to Ellis Island and New York City in the mid-1800s was the legendary Sarah Sands. For a time, my late father-in-law, an avid genealogist, believed that the Sands had transported my ancestors to America. I later determined that James and Eliza Bale did not sail on the Sands, but discovered that James and Lydia Bale did. The Sands' passenger manifest indicates that James, a 'smith', and Lydia, his wife, arrived on Ellis

Island in August of 1849, just a few weeks after the arrival of my great-great-grandfather. They all hailed from western England, and I suspect that the two James Bales were distant cousins.

Built by James Hodgeon and Company and registered in Liverpool, England, on December 19, 1846, the Sarah Sands was also a modest ocean-going vessel. But in contrast to the Unicorn, the Sands had four masts, rather than three, and her steam engine, made by Bury, Curtis, and Kennedy, a company known for its steam locomotives, drove a single screw propeller rather than paddle wheels. With a length of 207 feet, a beam of 30 feet, and a gross tonnage of 1,229, the Sands, somewhat larger than the Unicorn, could accommodate 300 passengers in first, second, and steerage classes. Originally designed for travel between the UK and Australia, the Sands sailed instead between Liverpool, England, and New York City, making her maiden voyage in January of 1847. She boasted a top speed of nine knots, enabling the Sands to make the 3300-mile voyage between Liverpool and New York in approximately 21 days.

Albert dock, Liverpool, England, present day
Source: The author

When my wife and I visited Liverpool's Maritime Museum, I learned that the principal owner of the Sands at the time of its maiden voyage was Thomas Sands of Liverpool, England. Sands, who had served as the city's mayor in the 1840s, financed the building of the Sarah Sands and named the ship for his wife.

From the museum's docent, I also learned that a ship's ownership in the 1800s consisted of 64 equal shares. The museum's archives revealed that the subscribing (investing) owners of the Sarah Sands included Thomas Sands, whose occupation was listed as merchant, with 16 shares; Charles Oddie, another merchant, with 10; and William Corseaden Thompson, the Master Mariner, with five. The remaining 33 shares were divided among seven additional merchants (24 total shares), a broker (five shares), the sailmaker (three shares), and an engineer (one share).

The Sarah Sands sailed from Liverpool to New York until the fall of 1849, not long after James and Lydia completed their voyage, when the Empire City Line chartered her for service between San Francisco and Panama. After a brief stint with the Empire City Line, the Sands returned to Liverpool, where she steamed between New York and her home port for one more season. In 1852, she plied the waters from Liverpool to Sydney, Australia, for the Melbourne Gold Mining Association, and in 1853, the Sands again steamed the Atlantic Ocean, this time for the Canadian Steam Navigation Company. I never learned the reasons for the many changes in the Sands' routes and ownership. Did they mean that the Sarah Sands was a desirable commodity or a liability?

When the Crimean War began in the fall of 1853, the English government appropriated the Sands and refitted her to transport troops from England to the Black Sea and the Crimean Peninsula. Triggered by religious beliefs and territorial conflicts, the Crimean War pitted the Russian Empire against the Ottoman Empire and her French and British allies. In all, more than 100,000 troops would perish, many due to the primitive management of the gruesome wounds caused by sabers and the crude firearms of the 19th century. And more than 500,000 additional soldiers would succumb to malnutrition or the infections they contracted in their crowded, unsanitary quarters.

The Crimean War, while unbelievably horrific, inspired Tennyson to write the patriotic poem *The Charge of the Light Brigade*, and the rigors of warfare gave us the balaclava, a cap knitted for the British troops by the women of England. Worn under the helmet to help keep a soldier warm, the wool cap received its name following the Battle of Balaclava in the late fall of 1854. In early 2024, my wife and I would learn firsthand the benefits of balaclavas when we traveled to frigid Antarctica. But most notably, the Crimean War set the stage for the remarkable exploits of Florence Nightingale.

Florence Nightingale spent her early childhood at family estates, Lea Hurst in Derbyshire, central England, and Embley Park in Hampshire, south-central England. Upon inheriting the Lea Hurst estate from Peter Nightingale, a great-uncle, Florence's father, William Edward Shore, changed his surname from Shore to Nightingale. Intelligent, precocious, and fiercely independent, Florence Nightingale, whose given name celebrated her birth in Florence, Italy, received her nursing education at the Institution of Protestant Deaconesses at Kaiserswerth, Germany, in 1850 and 1851. Later, she became the superintendent of the Institution for Sick Gentlewomen (*aka governesses*) in Distressed Circumstances in London before being called by the British Secretary of War in 1854 to serve the soldiers wounded in the Crimean War.

Accompanied by 38 women, Nightingale traveled to the British Army Hospital in Scutari, now known as Üsküdar, where she and her colleagues hoped to correct the wretched conditions that contributed to the unacceptably high mortality rates among the British soldiers wounded in the war. Florence Nightingale and the other nurses tended to the soldier's physical and emotional needs, and Nightingale's much-appreciated nightly hospital rounds earned her the sobriquet "the Lady with the Lamp." Her attention to hygiene and nutrition, as well as Nightingale's devotion to her patients, saved countless lives, and in the process, her work became the standard of care and professionalism for nursing and medicine in general.

Among the many nurses who cared for British soldiers during the Crimean War was Mary Seacole, a nurse/physician of Jamaican-Scottish ancestry. Having learned medicine as an apprentice to her mother, the owner of a boarding house for injured soldiers in Kingston, Jamaica, Mary Seacole sought permission from the British War Office to join Nightingale and her team of nurses in Crimea. When the War Office refused to send Seacole to Crimea, an affront that Seacole attributed to prejudice toward people of color, she used personal funds to support her own mission trip to Crimea in 1855. Once there, she founded the "British Hotel," described by Seacole herself as "comfortable quarters for sick and convalescent officers," near Balaclava, the site of intense fighting between the Russians and the British Allies. At her hotel, Seacole, like Nightingale, fed the soldiers and treated their many wounds.

Although I have scant information about James Bale's sisters, the family archives indicate that one of them, Rose Bale, was a nurse. A handwritten note on the photograph of Rose in her nursing attire states that she served in France with the British Expeditionary Forces during World War I. Although she was still alive during WWI, she would have been nearly 90 years old at the time. Thus, I believe that the handwritten information is incorrect. Service in Crimea, when Rose would have been in her early 30s, seems far more likely. Did Rose Bale serve with Nightingale or Seacole

Nurse Rose Bale
Source and Date Unknown

and travel to Crimea on the Sarah Sands? Or did they simply pass each other, much like ships in the night?

When the Crimean War ended, the Sarah Sands continued to transport British troops, this time from Plymouth, England, to Calcutta, India, during the Rebellion of 1857. The uprising challenged the power of the British East India Company, and although the rebellion did not achieve its objective, to create a sovereign state of India, the conflict ultimately led to the dissolution of the East India Company and the transfer of Indian rule to the British Crown, a pivotal event in India's 90-year quest for independence.

The East India Company chartered the Sands to ferry the troops from England to India, and she sailed from Portsmouth on August 15, 1857, carrying Her Majesty's 54th regiment, some 350 troops. Frederick Schlotel later wrote in a pithy 29-page narrative, *Burning of the Sarah Sands*, that England sent troops to battle the Sepoys (the native troops) and, in the words of Major-General W.Y. Moore, the regiment's commanding officer, "[to] inflict well-deserved retribution for the atrocious deeds which were filling England with horror and dismay." The long, perilous voyage would take the crew and the soldiers south from England along the shores of France, Spain, and Portugal, past the bulge and the treacherous Skeleton Coast of West Africa, and around the Cape of Good Hope.

After nearly two months at sea, the Sarah Sands steamed into Cape Town, South Africa, to load fresh coal and provide shore leave for its sea-weary troops and sailors. She then continued her journey, heading to India via Ceylon, a British colony. In the afternoon of November 11, 1857, while approximately 800 miles from land, the Sands caught fire.

> A cry of "Fire!"—that most horrible of cries at sea—was raised . . . Measures were taken by the chief officer and carpenter to discover the cause of the alarm, and, upon opening the hatchways, the smouldering material which lay in the stern of the vessel burst forth in a blaze . . .
>
> Orders were given to take in all sail, and bring the ship hard to wind . . . Lengths of hose were fitted to the fire-engine, but the water ejected by it produced no appreciable effect on the flames . . .
>
> There were five ladies on board, who were dressing for dinner when the alarm of "Fire!" was given. They had only time to put on whatever came nearest to hand, blankets, etc. They were then put in a boat, provided with fresh water, and such provisions as could be obtained, and lowered to the water.

Schlotel continued:

> The bravery of the men confronting the flames which seemed every moment gaining upon them, and threatening their lives with increasing fury, was worthy of highest admiration. The calm resignation depicted in their countenances as they performed their monotonous but arduous duty was an indication of such courage and constancy as only brave souls are capable of exhibiting in times of peril.

Of gravest concern to Moore and his comrades were the highly-explosive munitions stored on board the Sands. If the fire reached the powder, all would be lost.

> The men of the Regiment succeeded in removing the powder from the Starboard Magazine, but despaired of being able to reach the ammunition in the Port Quarter . . . none knew how soon the flames might reach the ammunition. Nevertheless, volunteers were found to attempt to clear the Magazine.

Despite their heroic efforts, the soldiers were not able to retrieve all of the powder.

> Two large barrels of powder remained, which no exertions enabled them to reach. Nothing more could now be done. Those in the boats were told to pull beyond the reach of danger, as in the event of explosion, the foundering of the ship was momentarily expected . . . about 9 o'clock the fire blazed through the upper deck and volumes of flame ascended the mizen rigging. Soon the mast fell with a crash . . . now the fire took mastery . . .
> . . . the expected explosion took place with fearful

effect. The stern cabins (at least what was left of them) were blown yards into the air, and a part of the port quarter was blown out. The ammunition exploded with the brilliancy of multitudinous sky rockets, and while the flames were raging from the midships to the stern, gave to the vessel the appearance of a volcano in eruption . . . The concussion caused by the explosion was so great, the stern of the vessel dipped, and for a moment was under water, and all believed she would settle down with all on board.

Much to the amazement of Major-General Moore, his troops, and the terrified passengers, the Sarah Sands did not sink. Rather, the enormous volume of water pumped into the ship during the crew's frantic attempts to fight the fire eventually quelled the inferno. Only the iron hull, which saved the ship from total destruction, and her wooden lifeboats, which had been launched when the fire began, remained intact. Despite the chaos, the conflagration, and the frightful explosions, no hands had been lost!

Once the fire subsided, the crew and passengers directed their efforts toward survival. The commander's compass, sextant, and the few charts that survived the fire confirmed that the Sands was miles from the nearest land.

Those only who have been on board a ship in distress can realize the misery caused by privations such as the sufferers of the Sarah Sands disaster had to endure. Nearly all of the provisions had been destroyed. There was a cask of rum, the contents of which were dealt out sparingly, and a quarter cask of sherry, put on board by the owners of the vessel . . . which was consumed, and we're only too thankful it was in our possession, a barrel or two of salt beef, and one or two of flour; these were all the provisions left by the fire.

Starvation and dehydration were not the only perils facing the survivors of the fire and explosion.

> Sharks were seen all through the night playing round the ship . . . They took a great fancy to the occupants of the boats, which they were repeatedly seen endeavoring to upset with their tails, and as each individual gained a hold upon the gangway ladder, they made a rush in hope of obtaining a bite, after the manner smaller fish scramble to get a crumb thrown to them.

Though Schlotel described the scene with colorful hyperbole, the mere presence of sharks undoubtedly terrified the crew, the soldiers, and the women of the Sands.

Because the fire had destroyed the steering mechanisms, the crew rigged ropes to turn the massive rudder and steer the ship as it drifted with the prevailing winds. After many days, they finally saw land on the horizon--the islands of Mauritius.

> After we had been at sea, in great distress, for nearly a fortnight, to our inexpressible relief, we sighted, about four o'clock p.m., the Peak of Peterbot, causing much excitement and delight after so long imprisonment aboard a wreck . . . When morning came, we entered Port Louis and disembarked our men. The news of the dangers we had passed through spread like wildfire in the town, and the inhabitants prepared to give us an enthusiastic reception . . . Considering nearly all of the inhabitants of the island were French, it was very gratifying to receive so hearty a welcome, as it showed the kindly feelings they entertained, not only for us, but for our countrymen . . .

After recuperating from their ordeal, Major-General Moore and his troops boarded the ship Clarendon and continued their journey to Calcutta. En route, the Clarendon and her passengers encountered a cyclone, an experience that likely seemed trivial when compared with the horrific fire. Meanwhile, the Sarah Sands, consisting only of an iron hull and a skeleton of charred wood, was towed unceremoniously back to England, where she was rebuilt as a sailing vessel. It seems only fitting that the owners would remove the steam engine and coal bins that had caused the catastrophe. The Sarah Sands then sailed the Indian Ocean uneventfully for several more years until she foundered in April 1869 in the Laccadive Islands off the southwestern coast of India.

The saga of the Sarah Sands also captured the imagination of Rudyard Kipling, the legendary British author and winner of the 1907 Nobel Prize for literature. He described its burning in a collection of children's short stories entitled *Land and Sea Tales for Scouts and Guides*, published in 1923. In a style befitting a laureate, Kipling wrote:

> No one seemed to have much hope of saving the ship so long as the last of the powder was unaccounted for. Indeed, Captain Castles told an officer of the 54th that the game was up, and the officer replied, "We'll fight till we're driven overboard." It seemed he would be taken at his word, for just then the signaling powder and the ammunition-casks went up, and the ship seen from midships aft looked like one floating volcano.
>
> The cartridges spluttered like crackers, and cabin doors and timbers were shot up all over the deck, and two or three men were hurt. But—this is not in any official record just after the roar of it, when her stern was dipping deadly, and all believed the Sarah Sands was settling for her last lurch, some merry jester of the 54th cried, "Lights out," and the jovial captain shouted back, "All right! We'll keep the old woman afloat yet."

After what seemed like endless days at sea, James and Eliza reached the New World without incident. Soon thereafter, they traveled west from New York to Michigan where they would settle in Paw Paw, a small farming community in the southwest corner of the state. But why Paw Paw?

3

Paw Paw

The first James Bale, aka Grandpa Bale, date unknown
Source: Unknown Photographer

James and Eliza arrived in Michigan barely two decades after the first Europeans reached the locale that would become the village of Paw Paw. Rodney Hinkley had claimed farmland near a village site in 1832, and Pierce Barber had constructed a simple sawmill on the Paw Paw River in the same year. Within another year, John Agard opened a trading post, and Lyman Daniels built an inn and tavern. At the time, Indigenous people outnumbered white settlers, and wolves, bears, and panthers still roamed the West Michigan forests, including those along the Paw Paw River.

In contrast to Devonshire's rugged coastline and rolling pastures checkerboarded with stone fences, the village that would straddle the Paw Paw River sat amidst virgin pine and hardwood forests and post-glacial lakes and marshes.

The land favored not the raising of sheep, a common pursuit in the British Isles, but the planting of corn and beans and the growing of apples, cherries, strawberries, blueberries, and grapes. Concord grapes would support the economy of Paw Paw for decades and would help the Bale family survive the Great Depression.

By 1835, the tiny village, soon to be named Paw Paw, the Indigenous name for the fruit that grew along the river, contained the Hinkley home, the tavern, the store, the cabin of Dr. Enos Barrett, a sawmill, a turning shop, and two shanties. Not long thereafter, Craig Buys, Hinckley's brother-in-law, established the first blacksmith's shop, and a cobbler, another essential tradesman, arrived in 1836. In March 1837, the year in which Michigan achieved statehood, the village was incorporated, and within another decade, Paw Paw sported a clothing store, four grocery stores, five dry goods stores, and an equal number of drug stores, as well as increasing numbers of people.

I found no evidence that anyone with the Bale surname resided in Paw Paw or the nearby villages prior to James and Eliza's journey to West Michigan in 1849. Eliza may have had distant relatives in the area, as suggested by several crumbling headstones bearing Pugsley, Eliza's maiden name, in the Prospect Hill cemetery south of Paw Paw. But this is only a guess. For the most part, it seems likely that the newlyweds relied on each other, their new neighbors, and whatever money they had to establish a new life together in America.

In the burgeoning village of Paw Paw, James' talent as a carpenter enabled him to find work readily, and the Bales prospered. Paw Paw, the nearby communities of Lawton and Mattawan, and the farmsteads of Van Buren County witnessed steady growth in the latter half of the 19th century, accommodating new settlers from the British Isles, Scandinavia, and other parts of northern Europe. Consequently, men with James' skills were in high demand.

In the 1860s, James and Eliza purchased land east of Paw Paw along the St. Joseph Trail, a few miles west of the tiny village of Mattawan. Encompassing 160 acres—a quarter section—their land contained a forest of oak, beech, and pine, necessary resources for constructing a farmhouse, barns, and outbuildings, and a natural prairie conducive to the planting of corn, alfalfa, and soy beans. In 1867, James and Eliza finished renovating the farmhouse and moved into their new home on land they would name 'The Maples'. Over time, they would add to their holdings and expand the farm to a stately 215 acres.

The Bales raised chickens, pigs, and cows, and grew corn and alfalfa to feed them. They also found time to raise four children: three daughters, Mary Ann; Jane Eliza, known to all as Jennie; and Henrietta, better known as Etta; and a single son, Waldwin James, whom everyone called Wally. According to a gravestone I found more than a century later in the Prospect Hill cemetery, James and Eliza also had another child, a boy named Eaven, who had been born between Mary and Wally but died in 1853 at the age of five months.

Eaven Bale's headstone,
Prospect Hill
Cemetery
Source: The author

As was the case with his paternal aunts, Susan, Caroline, and Lena, and paternal grandfather, William, I could find no details about Eaven's death. Given his young age at the time of his death, I believe that crib death, an enigmatic disorder that we now call Sudden Infant Death Syndrome (SIDS), seems most likely. But I don't know this with certainty and must add the cause of Eaven's death to the growing list of unanswered questions about the Bale family.

No written or oral record tells me how his parents coped with the passing of Eaven, their first-born son. Knowing how my wife and I grieved after the stillbirth of our second son, James and Eliza must have carried Eaven's loss as a heavy burden throughout their child-bearing years and beyond. Did they harbor guilt for his death? Did friends and neighbors believe that smothering or neglect, commonly held explanations for infant deaths in the 1850s, led to Eaven's death? Did the friends and neighbors hold the Bales responsible?

Over time, the Bale's stature in the community grew, particularly at Paw Paw's Methodist-Episcopal Church, where James and Eliza served in many roles, and James became known throughout West Michigan as a talented architect and builder. At a certain point in his adult life, James grew a full beard, and as the years passed, the beard's color turned first to salt and pepper and then completely white. His friends and family undoubtedly remarked that the beard made him seem even more wise and trustworthy than he already was, so he never shaved again. The beard's eventual snow-white appearance more than justified his sobriquet, Grandpa Bale.

When members of the Methodist-Episcopal congregation decided to rebuild their church in the mid-1870s, they recruited Grandpa Bale to draft the design and supervise the construction of their new house of worship. Although he had no photographs, drawings, or blueprints from which to work, his vivid memory of Ilfracombe enabled him to recreate the sanctuary of his boyhood church.

Methodist-Episcopal Church, Paw Paw, ~1915
Source: Church Records

A feature article in the November 30, 1941, issue of the Kalamazoo (Michigan) Gazette, the region's major newspaper, celebrated his contributions. "Mr. Bale," the Gazette reporter wrote, "used almost entirely ideas brought from English churches to apply to the American structure . . . it is known that Bale was married in an English church. It is thought that perhaps sentiment incurred him to use the designs of the church since it was one of his last memories of England."

Creative and ambitious, Grandpa Bale collaborated with Anson E. Lapham of Chicago, Illinois, to invent a device for delivering and receiving mail pouches to and from moving trains. As described in the patent granted by the U.S. Patent Office on September 20, 1898, the device received an inbound pouch and dropped it into a 'suitable receptacle' and simultaneously delivered an outbound pouch as the mail car passed by. In 1899, the Patent Office of the Dominion of Canada, Ottawa, Canada, awarded Bale and Lapham a patent for the device's use by the Canadian railroads. A diagram of the Bale-Lapham device remains on file in the U.S. Patent Office (patent #611,094), and original copies of both patents have been preserved in the family archives.

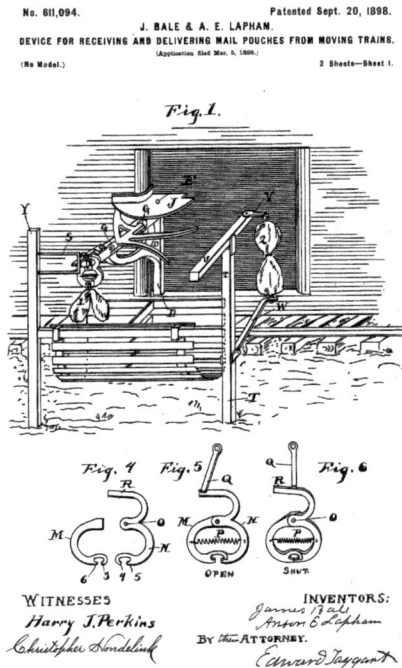

Bale-Lapham Patent, 1898
Source: U.S. Patent Office

Eliza would pass away in 1881 at the relatively young age of 56 years, and as is the case with many other family deaths, I do not know how she died. Nor, for that matter, do I know how Grandpa Bale met his second wife, Isabelle. Approximately one year after Eliza's death, Grandpa Bale married Isabelle McBain Chesebro of Grand Rapids, Michigan, a city approximately 50 miles north of Paw Paw. Could he have met Isabelle during a business trip to Grand Rapids? Did he build or remodel her home there?

Isabelle, 42 years old at the time of her marriage to Grandpa Bale, had been married previously to George J. S. Chesebro of Grand Rapids. A lovely young woman of Scottish heritage, Isabelle met George when she worked as a servant in the Chesebro household in Albany, New York. They married when she was just 16 years old; George was nearly a decade older at 25. Together, George and Isabelle had three children: Jennie, Crombie, and Grant.

Isabelle became a widow when George, who had been a school principal in Grand Rapids prior to the Civil War, died at 34 years of age in Goldsboro, North Carolina, on April 4, 1865, less than one week before Lee's surrender at Appomattox. Chesebro had served as a sergeant in the Union Army in Co. B. of the 1st Michigan Engineers & Mechanics under the command of Captains Baker Borden and John W. McCrath. As members of the Engineers Regiment, George and his fellow soldiers built bridges, railroads, and fortifications. Although they occasionally engaged in skirmishes with the Confederate Army, they carried muskets principally for their own defense. From the Regiment's total enrollment of 2920, only six would die from wounds sustained in conflict. A far greater number of the Regiment's soldiers, nearly 300, would succumb to disease, and George would be one.

Grandpa Bale and Isabelle lived together at The Maples until Isabelle's death from complications of kidney disease in 1901. Grandpa Bale would outlive Isabelle by another 17 years, and he died peacefully at the farm in 1918. With Grandpa Bale's passing, his son Wally inherited the farm and other Bale assets. A hand-written note I found hidden in the secret compartment of a portable writing box recorded the details of this transaction and described the holdings of the Bale family. In a true sense, the document served as a holographic will, written in Grandpa Bale's own hand to convey his assets to Wally, his only son. Among the farm's holdings were a beloved team of horses, some stock, the farmhouse, a barn, several outbuildings, and numerous bushels of corn and alfalfa. The farm had prospered during Grandpa Bale's ownership, and Wally would prove to be an equally capable steward of the Bale farm.

As was the tradition of the day, the daughters, Mary Ann, Etta, and Jennie, received only Grandpa Bale's unconditional love and his hope that they would marry well. Jennie, the youngest and my father's favorite aunt, never married, and spent, as did many youngest daughters, her entire life at her childhood home, caring for her aging parents. Jennie herself lived a full life of 94 years and passed away in 1948, not long before my own birth in January 1949.

Wally married Clara Belle Sheldon, and together they had two children, Beatrice Evelyn and James Sheldon. After a successful career as a farmer, Wally died at the age of 74, and he passed the Bale farm, as was the custom, to his only son, James Sheldon Bale, my grandfather. James' sister, Beatrice, known to everyone as 'Aunt Bea', married into the Thornton family and moved to Lawton, Michigan, just a few miles west of the Bale farmstead. Having learned the trade well from her father and grandfather, she farmed there with her husband, Hale Sr., raising dairy cattle and growing Concord grapes, which they sold to the Welch's juice plant in Lawton. Clara continued to live at The Maples until her own passing at the age of 91.

Clara's family history, a compelling story in its own right, dates from the 1600s, when an ancestor, William Sheldon, born in 1611, traveled to America with his three brothers, Isaac, John, and Godfrey, from Essex, England, to Dorchester, Massachusetts. They sailed on board a ship allegedly confiscated from the legendary British explorer and notorious privateer, Sir Walter Raleigh, who had been found guilty of treason after James 1 succeeded Queen Elizabeth 1. King James imprisoned Raleigh in the Tower of London for more than a decade, and for his alleged crimes, Raleigh was beheaded in 1618.

William Sheldon settled in Salem, Massachusetts, in the early 1600s. A descendant, Benjamin Gideon Sheldon, born in 1727, co-founded Stephentown, a village east of Albany in the scenic hill country of Rensselaer County near the New York-Massachusetts border. In the fall of 2023, my wife and I would visit the area and search the local cemeteries for my ancestor's headstones.

Although the city of Paw Paw demolished Grandpa Bale's beloved Methodist-Episcopal church late in the 20th century, his influence on our family persists, not just in the cherished documents and photographs held in the family archives but in the talents and imagination of each generation of the Bale family. When my cousin, a gifted athlete and accomplished high school teacher and coach, won a prestigious Fulbright Scholarship to study in England in the 1970s, the family story drew him to Ilfracombe in the hope that he would locate our relatives. Much to his initial surprise and eventual dismay, he discovered so many people with the Bale surname that he could not identify any relatives with certainty.

Stephentown, New York, present day
Source: The author

4

The Maples: Part 1

The Bale farm lies a few miles west of Mattawan, Michigan, at the corner of 27th Street and Red Arrow Highway, a two-lane highway that was once US 12, the major east-west route from Detroit to Chicago. The 'Red Arrow' designation honors the 32nd Infantry, the Red Arrow Division, composed of the Michigan and Wisconsin Army National Guardsmen who fought in World War I and World War II.

As boys, my brother and I would lie on a grassy knoll just above Red Arrow Highway and watch the cars as they sped by The Maples. We sometimes competed to see who would be the first to identify the makes and models. Before long, we could recognize the distinct differences between the Ford, Chrysler, and General Motors automobiles, the 'Big Three' of the day, as well as the subtle features that distinguished the Ford, Mercury, Lincoln, Dodge, Plymouth, Chrysler, Chevrolet, Buick, Pontiac, Oldsmobile, and Cadillac brands. We even knew the Studebakers and Nash Ramblers! Although my brother was nearly five years younger, he often won the day's contest. Years later, he purchased a vintage Chevy Corvair and spent many hours trying to get the car in running condition. To this day, I don't know if he ever did.

Because the Bale family once owned the land on all sides of the corner of 27th Avenue and Red Arrow Highway, locals knew the spot as Bale's Corner. When I was 12 years old, my mother sent me alone by Greyhound bus to spend a summer weekend at Grandma's house. As I boarded the bus, she instructed me to tell the driver to drop me off at Bale's Corner. When I told him, he knew exactly what it meant, and he stopped right on cue. Sometime in the distant past, the family sold the property on the east side of 27th Avenue but kept the Victorian house, barns, and land to the west and the farmland and woodlots to the south. I never learned exactly when they sold the property or what prompted the sale, but I often wondered if the Great Depression was the reason.

The difficult times of the Great Depression took a grim toll on Michigan farm families, including the Bales. When I once asked my dad, a schoolboy during the Depression, what he remembered of the 1920s and 1930s, he could only respond with the words "sadness . . . intense sadness." Because of the anguish in his voice, I never dared ask him about the Bale family's finances during the Depression or if the Depression contributed to the events that would take the life of his father.

The original farmhouse, erected by an unknown builder in the mid-1800s, was a simple, rectangular clapboard structure that measured no more than twenty by thirty feet. The house's three tiny rooms consisted of a parlor, a kitchen with a sink and hand-pump, and a sleeping room with just enough space for an oak dresser and a three-quarter bed. But the house had 'good bones', sitting on solid footings constructed of glacial boulders that had been retrieved from the surrounding fields. Not only did the boulders give the small home a sound foundation, their removal from the fields saved many an iron plow. In the mid-1860s, James and Eliza purchased the property and moved there with their children.

Soon after purchasing the farm, Grandpa Bale began an extensive two-year remodeling project that would transform the humble farmhouse into a stately, two-story Victorian showplace. He first dug a Michigan basement beneath the kitchen and bedroom to create cold storage for the curing of meat and the safekeeping of vegetables grown in the family's garden. In the process, he excavated the building's shallow crawlspace to a depth of about 6 feet, just deep enough to prevent most people from bumping their heads on the two-inch-wide, rough-sawn beams that supported the house above. He lined the walls with mortar to discourage cave-ins but left the floor bare to capitalize on the cool temperatures emanating from the earth below. Two wood-framed glass windows allowed just the right amount of sunlight to enter the otherwise dark and foreboding space.

Rather than demolish the original structure, he built the new rooms around and above it. He constructed a new kitchen, a spacious dining room, a larger parlor, and an additional bedroom on the main floor and designed a steep, central stairway that ascended to a second floor with five rooms, including a large master bedroom with a walk-in closet, three more bedrooms, and a storeroom. Ten-foot ceilings on the main floor and eight-foot ceilings upstairs added to the expansive feel of the new house.

The original builder clearly understood the benefits of the house's orientation. The kitchen on the north side blocked the frigid winds of winter, and the south-facing parlor provided the occupants with sunshine in the winter and shade in the summer. To capitalize further on the warmth of the winter sun, Grandpa Bale built a large bay window in the new parlor, and in the master bedroom, he designed an arched, west-facing window that captured the golden glow of the Michigan sunsets.

Master bedroom window, present day
Source: The author

Five interior doors connected the old rooms with those of the new house. Some doors now seem oddly placed, as if a committee had remodeled the farmhouse rather than a single builder. One door, later blocked by a large bookcase, entered the old home at the base of the new stairway, and another, soon permanently locked for safety, opened to the landing of the basement stairwell. The most logical of the doorways joined the two kitchens, enabling the old space, distant from the dining room, to be used as a summer kitchen when the days grew too hot and humid to cook comfortably in the new, larger kitchen.

The new home had two outhouses, a conventional one in the backyard behind a tall, barn-red corn crib, and the other, a two-seater, just inside the house in a large mudroom off the back porch. My dad chuckled when he described the Bale's 'indoor plumbing' since having an outhouse indoors meant that the family no longer needed to trudge through deep snow to 'do their business' during the winter. Fortunately, Grandpa Bale dug the pits deep enough to keep any unpleasant odors at bay. Each upstairs bedroom had a conveniently placed chamber pot.

Three large, covered porches, each with a tall entry door, added to the home's ample living space. The east-facing porch, shaded by the house itself, provided relief from the hot summer sun, while the open back porch adjacent to the kitchen afforded expansive views of the farm fields to the north. Later, the back porch would be screened to protect the Bale family and their guests from the pesky black flies and mosquitoes that thrived in the adjacent wetlands. At some point, a hired hand dug a shallow ditch to drain the largest of the swampy areas, one-quarter mile south of the farmhouse, and the nuisance of the mosquitoes abated.

In total, the house had five entry doors, two on the north side and one each on the east, west, and south. The front door and its vestibule opened to a semi-circular southern porch or portico, which was more decorative than functional, since most guests entered the Bale home via the back porch adjacent to the gravel driveway on the north. A final exterior door, added for emergencies, exited west from the dining room onto a concrete stoop and two steps leading to the grassy side lawn.

Grandpa Bale's early life in Ilfracombe during the reign of Queen Victoria, a beloved monarch who ruled the British Empire from 1837 to

1901, inspired the design of the new farmhouse. The Victorian era, characterized by rapid industrial and cultural progress, brought dramatic changes in both residential and commercial architecture. In contrast to the dull symmetry of utilitarian Georgian and Federal buildings, the vibrant architecture of the Victoria era, which encompassed Gothic Revival, Queen Anne, and Romanesque styles, celebrated asymmetry and embellishment. Style superseded function.

The Bale farmhouse, viewed from the east, date unknown
Source: Unknown photographer

As opposed to the square, flat roofs and horizontal lines that characterized Georgian or Federal houses, Victorian homes, as illustrated by the Gothic Revival style, embraced verticality with tall, steep roofs and turrets, often accentuated by pointed dormers. A Victorian home's elaborate elements could include bay windows, dentils, gingerbread trim, towers, and ornamental fretwork.

As Grandpa Bale began to remodel the farmhouse, he incorporated

Victorian influences by creating fancy but sturdy columns that supported the roof of the east porch, and crisscrossing decorative fretwork that graced the soffits above each of the double-hung windows on the second floor. Gingerbread moldings adorned the exteriors of the upstairs windows, and additional latticework embellished the front porch above the balusters of the wood railings. He carved an intricate sunburst design into the pine flooring of the front porch and decorated the overlying wood ceiling with its mirror image. Grandpa Bale wisely made the north porch, inconspicuous to those traveling past the farmhouse on Red Arrow Highway, sturdy and largely Georgian.

Gingerbread molding and decorative fretwork above a second floor window, present day.
Source: The author

He used hand tools to craft the moldings, the trim, and the heavy, four-panel oak doors, which he hung by hand throughout the remodeled house. French doors, placed between the parlor and dining room, allowed the sunlight from the parlor's expansive bay window to brighten both rooms. A large pocket door separated the front vestibule from the dining room and formed a thermal envelope, which helped insulate the living areas during the cold winter months. To assist those climbing the steep stairway to the upper bedrooms, he attached a sturdy, hand-milled oak railing to the east wall.

As the home's crowning feature, he created a massive, built-in hutch that filled the entire north wall of the dining room. Crafted from oak and ash, the ornate cupboard's cabinets and drawers provided ample storage space for dishes, silverware, and linens. In the middle section of the hutch, Grandpa Bale added an unobtrusive, two-by-two-foot opening with a vertical sliding door that enabled the cooks in the kitchen to pass food discretely to the dining room without disturbing the diners.

At some point, a small bathroom was added between the parlor of the old farmhouse and the first-floor bedroom. Constructed with two entry doors, much like a 'Jack and Jill' bathroom, the room contained a porcelain tub, wall sink, and toilet. One entry door led from the tiny bedroom in which my grandmother slept alone after her husband, my grandfather, died.

When we visited the farm with our parents in the 1950s and 1960s, my brother and I slept together in the first bedroom at the top of the stairs in an antique oak bed with a tall headboard ornately carved with acorns and oak leaves. The bed, a Victorian piece, had been in the family for nearly one hundred years. Dad said that the bed had been Aunt Jennie's, and his eyes momentarily glistened with tears when he told us. But then he smiled and added, "She lived a good life."

The bedroom, although not much more than 10 feet by 12 feet in size, felt large and airy due to the two east-facing windows that captured the morning sunlight. The room itself had sufficient space for the bed, a three-drawer oak dresser of similar vintage, a single pressed back chair, and a chamber pot that sat on the floor in a back corner. The bed's mattress, nearly as old as the bed itself, sagged toward the middle, creating a deep furrow in which Aunt Jennie had likely slept each night. She was a petite woman, unlike her nephew James, Dad's father. The bed and its mattress suited Mike and me just fine.

My brother and I avoided the chamber pot, however, mostly because Dad wanted us to empty it each morning. Instead, we chose to venture down the steep, central staircase to the first floor, where we would use the bathroom, which had been added when Grandma Bale remodeled the kitchen and mudroom in 1957. We descended the stairs cautiously, especially at night, since the steps were short and the risers tall, neither of which could pass current construction codes. Fortunately, we never slipped or fell, our bare feet successfully navigating each step.

Like many builders of the day, Grandpa Bale served as the architect, framer, roofer, plasterer, finish carpenter, and painter. To my knowledge, he had no blueprints, suggesting that Grandpa Bale relied on his creativity and keen spatial perception to design and build the farmhouse. Nor do I know if he hired laborers or recruited friends and neighbors to assist him. After completing the farmhouse in 1867, he built fine Victorian homes in Grand Rapids, Michigan's second-largest city, as well as elaborate cottages on picturesque Boot Island, an isle in northern Lake Huron shaped, as the name suggests, like a boot. The capstone of Grandpa Bale's successful architectural career, many would say, was Paw Paw's Methodist-Episcopal Church.

A Boot Island cottage designed and built by Grandpa Bale, date unknown
Source: Unknown photographer

When my father died in 1997, I inherited Grandpa Bale's tool chest and many of his tools. Constructed of pine, oak, and walnut boards, the dovetailed chest measures forty-one inches long and twenty-one inches wide and tall. Although termites had riddled the bottom's pine boards with holes during the chest's decades-long storage in a rarely-used outbuilding at the Bale farm, the pine sides, walnut top, and oak trim escaped unscathed. On one end are the words "J. Bale, Mattawan, Mich" which directed the chest's transatlantic shipment from England to Mattawan, the tiny village not far from the farm.

The chest's interior contains three nesting walnut trays, with the top tray covered by a brass-hinged walnut lid; each tray has compartments for hand tools such as awls, screwdrivers, chisels, and files. Another covered compartment fills the front side of the chest's interior and contains several slots for rip and crosscut saws. On the underside of the chest's walnut lid are diamond-shaped inlays of burled maple. Matching maple inlays embellish the walnut lids of both the top tray and saw compartment.

Grandpa Bale's tool chest, exterior, present day
Source: The author

I do not know who constructed the ornate but functional tool chest. Was it his father's prized possession, or did Grandpa Bale build it himself? Given his remarkable skill as a woodworker, it seems likely that

Grandpa Bale designed and built the fine chest to organize and protect the tools for their passage from England to America.

When I first opened the tool chest and spread its contents on the farm's lawn, I discovered that it contained numerous block and molding planes and one plough plane, in addition to many other hand tools. In all, the chest contained more than thirty planes. Grandpa Bale had used the tools and planes, constructed of iron and dense oak, rock maple, or beech, to fabricate the home's baseboards, railings, and interior trim, as well as the adornments for the built-ins, such as the elaborate hutch in the dining room.

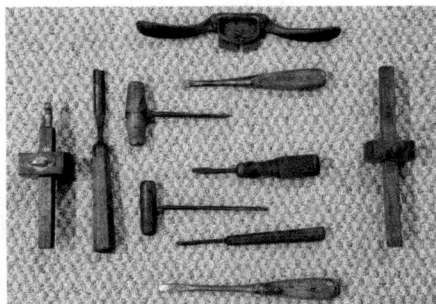

Some of Grandpa Bale's hand tools
Source: The author

The manufacturer marks indicate that the planes were made in England or the U.S. English tools included those manufactured by the Stothert Company, Bath, England, in the early 19th century; Cox and Luckman, Birmingham, England, in the mid-1800s; JB Bridge, date unknown; and Taylor and Son, Liverpool, England, date unknown. The U.S. tools were made by Benton Evans of Rochester, NY, in a narrow time frame between 1834 and 1838; H. Wells of Williamsburg, MA, around 1850; and the Ohio Tool Company, founded in Columbus, OH, in 1851.

Grandpa Bale owned many more planes and hand tools, but because their marks are absent or indistinct, I cannot determine their provenance. I never learned exactly how Grandpa Bale acquired the tools, but I suspect that he inherited some from his father and likely purchased others, as necessary, when he began to renovate the farm-house and construct other structures in West Michigan.

Over time, Grandpa Bale built a large barn and six outbuildings, including three substantial corn cribs, a pigsty, and a storage shed that once served as the ice house. One building was a garage-like shed that housed buggies in the early days and automobiles later, such as Grandma Bale's 1952 Ford V8 sedan that transported me to a Kalamazoo hospital for stitches when I was four years old.

Inspired by the propeller-driven airplanes I often saw flying overhead between Chicago and Detroit, I decided to ride my tricycle off the front porch and launch myself into the air. Gravity prevailed, and after my crash landing on the concrete steps, I sported an ugly gash in my forehead. Thank goodness for Grandma's faithful Ford!

A small shed, west of the farmhouse, which likely functioned as the ice house
Source: the author

The Bales also built a small hen house. While not a separate building like the others, the makeshift chicken coop was a cantilevered structure that extended west from the buggy shed and provided shelter for the egg-laying hens. Except for the house and the main barn, the structures were humble in comparison to those of several neighboring farms, and with the exception of the house, garage, and storage shed, all had been painted barn red. Strategically placed to the north and west of the farmhouse, the barn and larger outbuildings sheltered the house from the prevailing winds.

The large barn, situated thirty paces or so northeast of the back porch, had three parts: a front section with several stalls for milking cows; a generous middle section for wagons, tractors, plows, and other large farm implements; and an immense hay loft, the third section, which extended from the rear of the building forward and upward over both the middle and milking sections. When my brother and I were young, the large loft entertained us as an exhilarating, albeit dangerous, place for endless games of hide-and-seek.

During our visits to the farm, I frequently explored the large barn, searching for hidden treasure in every nook and cranny. My many explorations eventually etched the pungent aroma of the family's barn permanently into my memory. Decades later, while walking through the Hubbell Trading Post National Historic Site near Ganado, Arizona, the earthy smell of the Hubbell barn and its stock evoked a sudden, vivid flashback. In an instant, I was a young boy again, standing near a milking stall in the Bale barn.

Around the age of ten, I discovered the real treasure, Confederate currency. I found the bills at the bottom of a dusty chest that sat in a dark corner of the barn's front section. I would later learn that my grandma's grandfather, a Union Army officer, brought several bills back to the farm as souvenirs of the civil war. When I excitedly told my dad about the discovery, he responded dismissively with the revelation that he and his sister had often used the money to play store when they were young. He knew full well the treasures and memories that the barn held.

To the east of the large barn stood a tall silo, painted red with white trim to match the barn. Although silos come in many configurations, the Bale silo had the traditional tower shape and stood immediately adjacent to the barn. I never found treasure there, even though my dad had convinced me when I was young that farmers stored their money in the silos. I realize now that his words contained more fact than fiction.

Silos, derived from the Greek word *siros*, meaning pits for storing grain, protect one of the farmer's most precious products, silage. Silage, the food for sheep and cattle, is composed of alfalfa, clover, oats, or rye. Harvested when green and moist, the grasses are loaded into an airtight silo by a blower and allowed to ferment. Fermentation begins almost immediately, and within two weeks, the mature silage can be used as fodder. The sweet, intoxicating aroma of fermented silage, which permeated the silo and adjoining barn, undoubtedly accounts for the intensity of my childhood memories.

The 'House on Fire' granary, southeast Utah, present day
Source: The author

Silos can also be used to store harvested, or threshed, grain, and when put to this purpose, they are called 'grain elevators' or 'granaries'. Granaries have been used for centuries, and those dating from prehistoric times can be found throughout the desert southwest as remnants of both the Fremont and Ancestral Puebloan cultures. Made from mud and stacked sandstone blocks, the simple structures protected the ancient people's grain from wild animals and other people. Modern grain elevators, constructed from steel, aluminum, or concrete, store air-dried grain and prevent mold, another serious threat, from destroying the farmer's valuable harvest.

The Bale's smaller barn, constructed of oak and pine timbers joined by hand-hewn hardwood pegs, had a dusty dirt floor and two thick wood plank doors that swung to the west on hinges of hand-wrought iron. Over the years, the hinges sagged from the weight of the heavy doors, and the doors hung low, carving deep furrows in the soft earth upon which the barn rested. Opening them took the combined effort of vigorous pulling and heavy lifting, and not until my teen years could I open them without assistance. The walls sat on a low stone foundation, and irregular gaps in the weathered side walls revealed where mice and other rodents had gnawed the boards while searching for food and shelter. Inside the barn hung scythes, axes, rakes, hoes, shovels, and other hand implements.

More of a large shed than a barn, the building was already old when great-grandfather Wally purchased it from a neighbor more than one hundred years ago. The price was the labor of dismantling the building and hauling the wood and iron fittings to our farm. Wally did so carefully, board-by-board and hinge-by-hinge, and then he re-erected the structure on the Bale property using the same wooden pegs that had held the barn's beams and rafters securely for countless years. He chose the location wisely, avoiding the grape vineyard to the west and the stately row of tall pines planted by his father.

I nearly wept when my dad razed the small barn in the early 1970s and had the wood and iron carted away. He told me that he had to remove it before it collapsed and injured someone. I often suspected, however, that he needed to remove the building not because of any liability concerns but because it held too many disturbing memories. Like his grandfather, Dad bartered the sale price to the labor of dismantling the barn, removing the remnants, and leveling the ground upon which the building had once stood. This time, however, the buyer did not resurrect the barn but sold the iron as scrap and offered the weathered gray barn wood to artisans and antique dealers. To me, the removal of the old barn was a tragic loss, made even worse when Dad erected a sterile pole barn in its stead. Removing the wood barn and replacing it with an aluminum pole barn was like trading a vintage Corvette for a Chevy Vega.

In 1957, the farmhouse underwent a second major remodeling project when Grandmother Bale and Aunt Claribel hired men to bore a new well and lay pipes that brought running water to the kitchen and bathrooms. Carpenters installed plywood cabinets, which they painted white, and Formica countertops in the kitchen, and then laid vinyl flooring in the kitchen and new bath. Finally, they replaced the antique wood-burning stove with a natural gas stove and oven. Seeing the wood stove go was a bittersweet sign of progress. Whenever I ventured too close as a toddler, my grandmother would warn, "Hot Jimmy," and usher me away from the stove. How Grandma smiled when "hot" became one of my first words!

A new bathroom, separated from the kitchen and living areas by a 2-foot wide, vinyl accordion door, made the two outhouses obsolete. The outdoor privy was dismantled, and the pit was summarily covered with dirt. The workmen filled the pit of the two-seater indoor outhouse with a healthy amount of packed soil to eliminate any lingering odors, and carpenters sealed the openings with thick oak planks that later became part of a massive storage cupboard that occupied a good portion of the backroom.

The house would remain in this condition for another forty years until my mother moved to the farm from Rockford, Michigan, after my father died. Living alone and desperate for a distraction, she renovated the entire north end of the farmhouse. In the process, she used much of her life's savings to transform the old back porch, backroom, kitchen, and bathroom into a country kitchen with a sitting area and fireplace. There, she spent her days knitting, writing letters to her grandchildren, and doting on her beloved cat, Job, a stray that Mom had adopted while living in Florida.

Long before Mom moved to the farm, the large barn had collapsed, mostly from neglect. Dad eventually demolished what remained and had the debris hauled away. He replaced the barn with another aluminum pole barn. In contrast to the removal of the small barn, the large barn's demolition was fully justified, given what had happened years earlier behind its north wall.

The Bale farmhouse viewed from the southwest, present day
Source: The author

5

The Maples: Part 2

The farmhouse and pole barns now occupy approximately two of the 160 acres currently owned by the Bales. Of the non-residential land, woodlots cover approximately 30 acres, and the remaining acreage, leased to local farmers, has been sown with rotating crops of corn, beans, and alfalfa. The vineyard, removed by my grandmother in the late 1970s, once occupied about 10 of the tillable acres. To the west of the farmhouse, Grandpa Bale planted a long row of pine trees, and to the north, he planted a small grove of catalpas, hardy deciduous trees with unique, string bean-like seed pods.

Encouraged by our mom, my brother and I spent long hours harvesting and shucking the catalpa 'beans'. We counted them, too, but had no inkling at the time what 'bean counting' actually meant. I later realized that the piles of seeds we collected and counted each year served no useful purpose other than to keep two young boys out of trouble. Decades earlier, Grandpa Bale cut some of the young catalpas for vineyard posts, his original reason for planting the trees, but left most to mature and grace the farm with their white, orchid-like flowers.

The red and silver maple saplings, which Grandpa Bale had planted along Red Arrow Highway and the drive leading to the back porch, thrived, and for years, the mature trees shaded the farmhouse and much of the yard. When fall arrived, my brother and I would rake the colorful leaves into mountainous piles, and then, running as fast as we could, we'd leap onto them, our squeals filling the autumn air. The wind would dislodge the maple seeds, and they'd flutter down like butterflies to join the leaves on the lawn. We would then collect the seeds and cast them windward, creating countless squadrons of miniature helicopters. On crisp autumn evenings, we'd sometimes line the gravel drive with the dry leaves, ignite them carefully, and roast marshmallows by moonlight.

To the west of the catalpas, two large hickory trees stood in the midst of acres of valuable farm land. For years, their presence forced the tractors to veer around them during the spring plantings and fall harvests. Whether the trees resulted from a forgotten squirrel cache or the work of a mischievous Bale youngster, no one knows for certain. I favor the former, given the abundance of fox, gray, and red squirrels that lived on the property. In the fall, my mom, brother, and I would hike to the trees and gather the hickory nuts from which we would extract the nutmeats for Mom's mouth-watering chocolate chip cookies.

Hickory trees northwest of the Bale farmhouse
Source: The author

A much more laborious process was needed to harvest the black walnuts that fell in huge quantities from the three tall walnut trees that stood just west of the farmhouse. Each tree could yield as many as 400 pounds of nuts annually. Covered with thick green husks, walnuts epitomize the adage 'a tough nut to crack', since harvesting the treasured nutmeats necessitated a time-consuming, multi-step process. In the initial phase, we'd toss the fully-husked walnuts onto the gravel drive and wait for the postman and other visitors to drive their vehicles over the nuts to dehull them. Sometimes, we'd even ask Dad to drive his Buick back and forth just to gain a few more. This essential step minimized our exposure to the inky resins that left indelible stains whenever we attempted to remove the husks by hand.

After several weeks of dehulling and drying in the driveway, the inner nutshells were collected, and we would spend long afternoons with hammers and sharp nutpicks, cracking the hard shells and harvesting the delicious nutmeats hidden inside. We sorted the nutmeats carefully, since contaminating them with a driveway stone or even the smallest fragment of their rock-hard shells could lead to a broken tooth. Once we finished our work with the shells, we bagged the nutmeats and stored them for later use.

Among my favorite black walnut recipes were Aunt Claribel's grape conserve and my mother's banana-nut bread. As for the bread, Mom typically made several loaves during the week before Thanksgiving dinner, and the tantalizing aroma of her baking would fill our kitchen for days. Had she not hidden the loaves well, the delicious bread would have been eaten long before the dinner. When the day finally arrived, she loaded the banana-nut bread and a freshly-baked apple or pumpkin pie into her wicker picnic basket and carted them to Aunt Bea's house, where we annually met for Thanksgiving dinner. Until I was 16 years old, I sat at the kid's table in the kitchen, and when we kids had exhausted our allotment of pies and banana-nut bread, we'd sneak a few more slices of each from the adult table in the dining room.

Every fall, the owners of nearby sawmills would stop and ask Grandma and later, my mother, if they could buy the walnut trees. Coveted by furniture makers and other craftsmen, each tree could bring as much as a few thousand dollars. Selling them, of course, meant their destruction, since a lumberjack would cut them down at ground level, discard the limbs, and leave behind ugly stumps as sad reminders of the trees' past glory. Fortunately, both Grandma and Mom declined the offers each year, despite the temporary wealth the trees would bring, and let the stately trees stand, providing shade and annual crops of walnuts sufficient for our needs and those of the squirrels that lived in harmony with the Bale family.

On the most southern end of the property stood the largest woodlot, approximately 20 acres in all. Comprised of scrub oak, beech, and pine, the copse provided shelter for deer, squirrels, rabbits, and wild turkeys. Later, coyotes began to populate the land around the farm, and they often wandered through our woodlots and farmland in search of small game. The presence of the coyotes worried our mom, not so much for her own safety, but for the welfare of her cat, Job. She kept a close eye on him, lest he bolt from the house through an open door and become a quick meal for a hungry coyote.

Woodlot south of Red Arrow Highway, present day
Source: The author

A shallow ditch drained the wetlands on the southern-most end of the Bale property and pro-vided cover whenever my dad and I scouted for white-tailed deer, an important protein source for many of the local farmers and their families. After a Sunday dinner at The Maples during their court-ship, Mom asked Dad if there was something wrong with the beef that his mother had served that evening.

"It seemed tainted, Jim," Mom had said.

Dad laughed as he confessed, "That was venison, Marilyn." The meal had been her first exposure to deer meat, and she vowed that night, as a condition of marriage, that it would also be her last.

To the west of the farmhouse, just beyond the pines that Grandpa Bale had planted to protect the house from the prevailing winds, stood the vineyard. There, Concord grapes grew in long, leafy rows on fence-like structures constructed of sturdy steel wine strung between catalpa-wood posts placed every twenty feet or so. Each spring, the vines would snake their way along the wires, and tiny clusters of green grapes would appear and gradually mature into deep purple fruit, nourished by the summer rains and ripened by the sunny days and cool nights of fall. Depending on the weather, the grapes could be ready for harvest as early as late August, but the best crops came when the frosts arrived late and the grapes matured into early October.

An aging, one-room shed similar to the structures that might have housed migrant farm workers
Source: The author

In the 1950s, many of Paw Paw's growers hired migrant laborers to harvest their grapes, and several of the larger growers constructed small cabins in which the laborers and their families lived during the annual fall harvests. Lacking heat and running water, the structures provided only modest shelter from the wind, rain, and chill of Michigan's unpredictable fall weather. The Bale vineyard, being smaller than most, employed day laborers who would arrive each morning to cut the compact grape clusters from the vines, place them into wood lugs stamped with the Welch name on each end, and stack the filled lugs in a side yard. There, the sweet aroma of ripe grapes would waft through the crisp fall air. When the day's harvest was complete, the laborers loaded the filled lugs onto a large flat-bed truck and hauled the crop to Welch's juice plant in Lawton.

Like tomatoes and corn, Concord grapes did not originate in the old world of Europe or Asia but in the new world of the Americas. Wild grapes, the fox grape (*Vitis labrusca*) and frost grape (*Vitis riparia*, also known as the riverbank grape), grew abundantly in the forests of

New England, and years of evolution endowed them with the ability to survive harsh winters and tolerate acidic soils inhospitable for the European wine grapes, *Vitis vinifera*. However, the wild grape clusters were sparse, and the fruit was tiny and tart.

A vintage wood Welch's grape lug, present day
Source: The author

In the late 1840s, the New Englander Ephraim Wales Bull began experimenting with wild grape plantings, and in 1853, after carefully evaluating numerous seedlings, he succeeded in cultivating a domesticated fox grape that produced abundant, sweet fruit on plants that still withstood the harsh New England growing conditions. Because Bull perfected the cultivar on his farm in Concord, Massachusetts, the grape, a variety of *Vitis labrusca*, became known as the Concord grape.

So far as we know, no Johnny Appleseed-like character brought the Concord grape from Massachusetts to Michigan. Appleseed, an alias for John Chapman, planted apple trees in numerous locations from Pennsylvania to Michigan, and when 50 tree seedlings emerged on a given plot of land, he could claim the land as a permanent homestead and sell it at a substantial profit. The entrepreneurial Chapman also planted apple trees to promote the production of hard cider, an alcoholic drink commonly consumed in colonial times.

Rebecca Rupp, a historian, once wrote that the typical Massachusetts adult of 1790 "drank approximately 34 gallons of beer and hard cider annually." Simple math indicates that these early Americans consumed nearly 3 gallons per month! Consumption of hard cider began to decline in the 1800s, and prohibition in the 1920s and early 1930s further curtailed the household production and use of hard cider in the

U.S. Apple orchards throughout the East and Midwest succumbed to the axes of the revenuers and the fires set by zealous supporters of the temperance movement.

Likely brought to the Midwest from New England by the early settlers, the Concord grape thrived in the sandy soils of southwest Michigan. The area's climate, moderated by the prevailing winds off Lake Michigan, the third largest of the Great Lakes, provided warm days, cool nights, and abundant precipitation, conditions favorable to the cultivation of grapes and other fruit. Although wine can be made from the Concord grape, as evidenced by the intermittent success of the wineries in Paw Paw and nearby communities, juice and jelly account for most of the popularity and profits of the Concord grape.

Concord grape vineyard near Lawton, Michigan, circa 2010
Source: The author

We owe much of the Concord grape's success to Dr. Thomas Welch, a dentist and Methodist minister who sought a non-alcoholic wine for his parishioners. Welch discovered that boiling the grape juice destroyed the yeasts that would otherwise turn the juice into wine and eventually into sour vinegar. Although the pleasing, sweet flavor of Welch's juice stimulated some domestic consumption, most of the early grape juice production of Welch and other competing factories was destined for communion tables as the 'Blood of Christ'.

Welch's son, Dr. Charles Welch, a dentist like his father but a far more imaginative entrepreneur, began to promote the secular consumption of grape juice in the late 1870s. He capitalized on the expanding temperance movement and an American health food obsession that would also contribute to the success of the cereal barons, Kellogg and Post, in Battle Creek, Michigan. The younger Dr. Welch took his juice, now named Welch's Grape Juice, to the 1893 Columbian Exposition in Chicago, Illinois, where thousands of visitors discovered its delicious flavor. His company flourished, and later, Welch would also promote grape juice for its beneficial health qualities.

Grape jelly, an additional Welch product, benefited not just from this visionary entrepreneur but also from the harsh realities of war. When the doughboys of World War I needed a ready source of energy to defeat the Germans, the U.S. government shipped tons of grape jelly, known then as Grapelade, to the front. Later, the popularity of Grapelade—which rhymes with marmalade—among returning veterans led to the second coming of Welch's company through its successful marketing of Welch's Grape Jelly.

Years later, when the GIs of World War II needed protein, the government sent peanut butter to the front so that the Allied soldiers could make peanut butter sandwiches. Grape jelly and peanut butter provided a nutritious source of carbohydrates and protein, so quite logically, peanut butter and jelly sandwiches became the efficient and effective energy boost the GIs needed as they headed to their next battle. PB&J sandwiches are far tastier, many would say, than the U.S. Army's subsequent creation, 'meals-ready-to-eat', aka MREs.

The emergence of peanut butter and jelly sandwiches as a staple item in American households required the convergence of three seminal events in the history of U.S. food production: the appearance of peanut butter at the same 1893 Columbian Exposition that witnessed the debut of grape juice; the WWI popularity of Grapelade; and the invention of the commercial bread slicer by Otto Frederick Rohwedder in 1927. When Dr. John Harvey Kellogg, the co-founder of Kellogg's Cereal Company, developed the process for making peanut butter and Dr. Ambrose Staub designed the first peanut butter manufacturing machine, the key ingredient of the PB&J sandwich, peanut butter, was ready. Thirty years later, Kellogg would write:

> It occurred to me that one of the objections to the extensive dietetic use of nuts might be overcome by mechanical preparation of the nut before serving it so as to reduce it to a smooth paste and thus insure the preparation for digestion which the average eater is prone to neglect. The result was a product which I called peanut butter.

The first recipe for a PB&J sandwich, attributed to Julia Davis Chandler, was published in the Boston Cooking School Magazine of Culinary Science and Domestic Economics in 1901. According to Sam Dean, a staff writer for *Bon Appétit* magazine, the sandwich was a "dainty affair," which Chandler described as follows:

> For variety, someday try making little sandwiches, or bread fingers, of three very thin layers of bread and two of filling, one of peanut paste, whatever brand you prefer, and currant or crab-apple jelly for the other. The combination is delicious, and, so far as I know, original.

Early on, only men and women of high society ate PB&J sandwiches, typically at afternoon teas or similar social occasions, but following WWII, commoners also discovered the delightful taste of peanut butter and jelly sandwiches. To this day, PB&Js remain the favorites of children and the young at heart everywhere.

As early as the 1890s, Dr. Charles Welch promoted the potential health benefits of the Concord grape and its juice, jelly, and jam. Years later, Katherine Zeratsky, a registered dietician and nutritionist at the Mayo Clinic in Rochester, Minnesota, would write that eating purple grapes, such as the Concord, could benefit a person's health by lowering the amount of circulating low-density lipoproteins (LDLs), the 'bad' cholesterols that influence the risk of heart attack or stroke. Purple grapes may also aid in preserving normal blood pressure, another factor that could reduce the likelihood of having a stroke or heart attack. Like blueberries, cranberries, strawberries, and citrus fruits, Concord grapes contain substantial amounts of flavonoids, the colorful plant chemicals that may reduce inflammation and cancer risk.

Freedman and colleagues reported in a 2001 issue of the respected medical journal *Circulation* that adults who drank Welch's purple grape juice for 14 days had a reduced tendency to form blood clots and had higher levels of nitric oxide, a circulating chemical that promotes relaxation of the arteries and improves blood flow. While the Freedman study can be criticized for its limited sample size and brief duration, the results nonetheless suggest that people who drink Concord grape juice could derive important health benefits, such as reducing the risk of heart attacks or strokes. So, how might this work?

Free radicals, atoms with a single electron, contribute to numerous degenerative processes in humans, including aging, Alzheimer disease, and atherosclerosis, colloquially known as 'hardening of the arteries.' Purple grapes, such as the Concord grape, contain large amounts of antioxidants, the chemicals that protect human cells from free radicals. So, by virtue of the biochemical interactions, juice from Concord grapes could block the deleterious effects of free radicals and, in turn, prevent disabling human conditions.

Although Dr. Kellogg, a Welch contemporary who was popularized in T. C. Boyle's fictional account, *The Road to Wellville*, did not extol the virtues of the Concord grape in his 1600 page tome, *Home Handbook of Hygiene and Medicine*, he did describe a "grape cure" for treating congestion of the lungs, a condition with cough, rapid breathing, and shortness of breath. The cure, which consists of the patient eating several pounds of grapes daily, can, to quote Kellogg, '[be] wonderfully successful'. Kellogg did not specify, however, the type of grape or the length of treatment. Did Kellogg embellish a result that may have only represented a placebo effect? Or do Concord grapes truly possess some remarkable therapeutic properties?

Otto Frederick Rohwedder, the final player in the emergence of the PB&J sandwich, initially encountered little interest in his invention, the mechanical bread slicer, when he presented it to Midwest bakers in the late 1920s. Born in 1880 in Davenport, Iowa, one of the 'quad cities' along the Mississippi River, fifty miles east of Iowa City, my home for 15 years, Rohwedder became a successful jeweler, an occupation that provided the resources and time to pursue his passion for inventing.

After nearly two decades of tinkering, Rohwedder perfected his slicing machine in 1927, only to have the Great Depression derail his plans to market the invention. He was ultimately forced to sell the invention and his patents to Micro-Westco Company in Bettendorf, Iowa, another of the quad cities, and become an employee of the company. In what seems like cruel irony, Rohwedder's first assignment as a salesman was to market his very own bread slicer. When another Iowan, Charles Strite, invented the pop-up toaster in 1921 and Wonder Bread appeared in 1930, sliced bread finally became the household staple that Rohwedder had envisioned.

My own connection with Rohwedder and Strite began with a

The Juice of the Concord is

MOST DELICIOUS

Puritan Grape Juice
Is the Acme of Perfection
NONE BETTER

Made Only By the
Paw Paw Grape Juice Co., Ltd.
Paw Paw, Michigan

Advertisement for Paw Paw grape juice, early 1900s
Source: The author

childhood fascination with the pop-up toaster and a passion for toast. When I was four years old and we lived in Buchanan, Michigan, where my mother worked for Clark Equipment, I toasted and buttered an entire loaf of sliced bread so that my parents could eat breakfast in bed on their wedding anniversary. Indeed, sliced bread was the real thing! Upon his retirement, Rohwedder moved to Michigan and further reduced our degrees of separation when he settled in Albion, my mother's birthplace, and lived his final days in Concord, Michigan, the home of my ancestors.

In all the years that I visited the farm at harvest time, I never saw Grandma Bale work in the vineyard. Aunt Claribel, on the other hand, loved to work with the men, cut grapes, fill lugs, and help load the Welch's trucks. Grandma often acted aloof toward the migrant workers, a behavior that seemed better suited for afternoon tea at the Drake Hotel in Chicago than for chores on the farm. By contrast, her sister, my Aunt Claribel, could work side-by-side with the men in the fields, laugh at their off-color jokes, and undoubtedly tell a few of her own in the process. While I never saw Aunt Claribel drink a bottle of beer or a shot of whiskey, I suspect that she could hold her own there, too!

Aunt Claribel, the feisty younger sister of grandmother Bale, kept the Bale family together, even when her own personal life seemed to be in shambles. She lived with her sister, Blanche, rather than with her husband, Uncle Fred, mostly because Fred, a wiry, handsome man and inveterate hoarder, had filled their Lawton home with his stuff, no matter its arcane purpose. Their relationship suffered, as well, from Fred's proclivity for procrastination. Several interior lath walls of their home lacked plaster, and marble for the fireplace hearth still sat in cardboard boxes on the living room floor, waiting for Fred to mix some mortar and lay the square stones. We visited the house occasionally but couldn't stay long, for we could find few empty chairs upon which to sit. Despite their prolonged separation, Aunt Claribel still loved Fred, I believe, and to the best of my knowledge, she never filed for divorce.

Aunt Claribel, a petite woman who stood barely four feet, eleven inches tall, and never topped 100 pounds, took most of this in stride and rolled with the hard knocks of life, much like the day she found a snake in the hen house. The snake, a nonpoisonous gopher snake, had coiled itself around a clutch of eggs, preparing to swallow them one by one. When Aunt Claribel reached up to collect the freshly laid eggs, she felt the snake. Rather than scream or run away in fright, she grabbed the squirming snake, yanked it out of the chicken coop, and promptly strangled it. She then grinned triumphantly as she tossed the dead snake over the back fence.

Though I admired Aunt Claribel's courage, I often felt sorry for the snake and thought of the poor fellow every time Aunt Claribel gave me a backrub. Her grip was like iron, hardened by her work in the vineyard and long hours cutting and packaging paper at a nearby factory. I never crossed Aunt Claribel, ever. Nor did I ever ask her about my grandfather. Had I asked, I suspect that she would have told me, for Claribel knew all of the family secrets and always spoke the truth.

Although they needed every dollar that the grapes brought, the Bales kept a portion of the grape harvest each year to make juice and jams. To make juice, Grandma and Aunt Claribel would simmer ripe grapes in water, add sugar to taste, fill quart-sized glass mason jars with the mixture, and then hot-pack the jars in a boiling water bath. The last, critical step killed any contaminating yeast spores, as Welch had learned years earlier, and prevented fermentation. Grandma and Aunt Claribel would store the jars in the Michigan basement to cure. To drink the prepared juice, we'd strain out the skins and seeds and enjoy the residual liquid, a juice far tastier than any store-bought product.

Of the jams they made at the farm, Aunt Claribel's grape conserve was by far my favorite. In a time-consuming process that typically took most of a day, she would separate the grape skins from the pulp and then cook the pulp to loosen the seeds. After passing the cooked pulp through a colander to remove the seeds, which she discarded into the trash pile behind the barn, she mixed the seedless pulp, the uncooked skins, finely chopped orange zest, tangy nutmeats from the black walnut trees, and just the right amount of sugar. She then boiled the mixture carefully until it reached the correct stage, poured the hot jam into half-pint jars, and, in a final, crucial step, sealed the jars with hot paraffin. Although laborious, the process yielded the most wonderful jam. Whenever my brother and I had been good, as judged exclusively by Aunt Claribel, she treated us to toasted Roman Meal bread spread with butter and generous layers of her mouth-watering conserve.

While the grapes provided the Bale family with money each fall, they relied heavily on corn, alfalfa, and beans as their principal cash crops. The handwritten letter that transferred ownership of the farm from Grandpa Bale to his son, Waldwin, in the late 1800s revealed the farm's true value. In addition to the detailed description of the farm's tangible assets, including buildings and livestock, the letter specified that each of the farm's 100 acres could yield up to 40 bushels of corn. With a bushel worth about $1 in 1880, the farm income from corn amounted to ~$4,000 annually, a handsome sum corresponding to more than $90,000 in today's dollars.

Although the amount seemed sufficient to meet the family's needs in the 1880s, farming never guaranteed a steady income. Take the dust bowl days, for example, when corn yields plummeted to less than 5 bushels per acre, if a crop could be grown at all. Michigan escaped the drought that ravaged eastern Colorado, most of Kansas, and the panhandles of Texas and Oklahoma in the 1930s, but not the record-setting summer heat. Michigan, along with Minnesota, Wisconsin, and the Dakotas, experienced their highest temperatures ever recorded in July 1936. The fields baked in the hot sun, and the corn withered, decimating farm incomes throughout the nation's heartland. Farming is a perilous business, indeed!

The adage 'behind every successful rancher is a wife who works in town' applies equally well to farmers. Grandma Bale's teaching career brought steady income to The Maples, but her passion to teach would also jeopardize her relationship with my grandfather.

6

Another James Bale

My dad, James Franklin Bale, the younger of the two children born to Blanche and James Sheldon Bale, entered the world on January 1, 1923, at Bronson Methodist Hospital in Kalamazoo. By just two hours, he missed being the first child born at Bronson in the New Year. Consequently, his parents did not receive the many gifts accorded to the lucky parents by the hospital. No matter, though. Blanche and James were undoubtedly delighted to have a healthy newborn son and potential heir for the Bale farm. Waiting for him at The Maples were Aunt Claribel and his five-year-old sister.

Little was recorded about Dad's early childhood. The few pictures I have show a thin, serious-looking child standing proudly with his mother, sister, and occasionally his father. He spent his early childhood like most farm boys, I suspect, doing chores, running errands, and periodically getting into trouble. As a young boy, he enjoyed sitting on the tractor with his father as he worked the fields, helping him sow seeds each spring and harvest crops the following fall.

Riding cautiously beside his father, my dad would sometimes find arrowheads on the Bale property, land that had once been the hunting grounds of the Miami, Ottawa, and Potawatomi people. Many of these Native Americans traveled the St. Joseph Trail, which bisected Van

Buren County in a route that would later become I-94, and in doing so, they frequently walked through the Bale property long before we would own the land.

Arrowheads found at The Maples
Source: The author

The St. Joseph Trail, one of three major east-west Indian footpaths crossing Michigan's Lower Peninsula, began at the western shore of Lake Erie near the present-day border of Michigan's Wayne and Monroe Counties. The trail, I learned, wound through virgin land westward toward Lake Michigan and the future site of the twin cities of Benton Harbor and St. Joseph, and in the process, the trail traversed much of southern Michigan through the present-day counties of Washtenaw, Jackson, Calhoun, Kalamazoo, Van Buren, and Berrien, a distance of approximately 150 miles. The footpath, rarely more than two feet wide, passed beneath towering white pine, beech, and maple, crossed numerous streams, and generally avoided the treacherous swamps that dotted Michigan's post-glacial landscape.

The Old Sauk and Grand River Trails, the other major east-west Indian footpaths of southern Michigan, mostly paralleled the St. Joseph Trail, although the Sauk Trail veered southwest through present-day Berrien County to enter land that would become Indiana. By contrast, the Grand River Trail angled northwest to end at Lake Michigan near the present-day city of Muskegon. The Grand River footpath, which followed the course of Michigan's longest river, would later be the route of I-96, another of Michigan's major interstate highways.

The Indigenous people also traveled north and south through the

Lower Peninsula along three other footpaths: the Cheboygan Trail, which connected land that would become Midland and Cheboygan Counties; the Mackinac Trail, which bisected the northern lower peninsula from present-day Midland to the Mackinac Straits; and the Shore Trail, which ran parallel to the western shore of Lake Huron through a wilderness that would eventually be the counties of Arenac, Iosco, Alcona, Alpena, and Presque Isle en route to the future townsite of Cheboygan, Michigan. These major footpaths joined other trails, including the Saginaw and Shiawassee footpaths, which facilitated travel to eastern Michigan and connected with other east-west trails. In all, more than a dozen major Native American footpaths crisscrossed Michigan's Lower Peninsula.

Philip P. Mason, a noted Michigan historian who taught at Wayne State University in Detroit, Michigan, wrote extensively about the footpaths of the Indigenous people and their impact on travel throughout Michigan's peninsulas. The footpaths, typically narrow and inconspicuous, traversed the Michigan wilderness, often following the courses of its many streams and rivers. The paths allowed travel between the Native settlements and to the forests and rivers that provided the Indigenous people with fish and game. Later, the same footpaths would be used by white settlers as they began to explore and populate the land that would become the State of Michigan. Through much effort, the footpaths gradually became horse trails and wagon roads, and over time, some would eventually become the routes of today's state highways and expressways.

Dad attended school in Paw Paw, while his mother, an elementary school teacher for more than 40 years, taught in rural Van Buren County or in Oshtemo, a village 15 miles east of Paw Paw on the outskirts of Kalamazoo. This arrangement circumvented the possibility that Dad or his mother would be accused of favoritism. A capable student, Dad did not excel in school and received mostly B grades with an occasional A or C. He seemed to be preoccupied with sports, girls, and other extracurricular activities. He loved basketball, and at an early age, he perfected an underhand free throw, a style later popularized by the legends of the National Basketball Association, Rick Berry and Wilt Chamberlain. Standing 5' 8" by 9th grade, my dad anticipated growing to over six feet tall like his athletic father, but his growth abruptly ceased, and he remained 5' 8" thereafter.

JIMMY BALE
PAW PAW

1940

Dad, age 17
Source: Paw Paw schools

Dad learned how to drive a car by the time he reached sixth grade, and like the farm kids of Iowa and the Dakotas, he could drive to school long before he could vote or legally buy a beer. He dated many girls before he met my mother, and a few relationships lasted longer than others. Some lasted only one date, like the time a horse nearly ended up in the front seat of his mother's Ford. Dad had not seen the horse crossing the county road that dark night until it was too late, and he broadsided the animal. Fortunately, his date, horrified and spattered with the horse's blood, was otherwise uninjured. The horse, which had broken free of its tether, did not fare as well and had to be destroyed.

Dad's parents believed in corporal punishment for a child's transgressions, but given his age at the time of the crash, the punishment consisted of earning enough money to repair the car and reimburse the farmer for the loss of his horse. The collision with the horse and his subsequent relationship with my mom-to-be had a sobering effect on Dad, and although Dad's passion for driving persisted, he generally avoided narrow country roads after dark, especially where horses might be lurking.

After graduating from high school in 1941, Dad attended Western

Michigan College of Education in Kalamazoo, where he would eventually receive a bachelor of science degree. When his father died suddenly in 1943, he left school to work on the farm and help his mother and aunt. Because he was an only son and needed on the farm, he received a draft deferment and avoided fighting in World War II. Dad bore a life-long guilt for the deferment, I believe, especially when many high school and college classmates fought with the U.S. Armed Forces in the European and Pacific theaters. And some never returned.

Dad did not enjoy farming, I suspect, and soon opted to become a teacher like his mother. Teachers were in short supply during and immediately after the war, and at the tender age of 19, he began teaching in a one-room, rural school not far from Paw Paw. In 1947, he returned to Western to complete an undergraduate degree in elementary education. He subsequently received a master's degree in education administration from the University of Michigan in the mid-1950s and remained forever loyal to the 'Big Blue' thereafter.

Dad had a marvelous, self-taught baritone voice with a range and mellow quality not unlike Bing Crosby's. While in college at Western Michigan University, he began singing with the Bendix Corporation Male Chorus of South Bend, Indiana. In the 1940s, numerous companies throughout the country sponsored male choruses, a phenomenon that began in the early 1900s and persisted through the first half of the 20th century, predating by many years the popularity of men's choruses during the AIDS epidemic.

Several sponsoring corporations existed within a fifty-mile radius of Paw Paw, including the Bendix Corporation, an automobile and aviation supply company based in South Bend, Indiana; the Studebaker Corporation, one of the Midwest's original automobile manufacturers, also based in South Bend; and Tyler Refrigeration, a Niles, Michigan, company that would dissolve during the Great Recession of 2008-2009. It was inevitable, given Dad's talent, that he would be recruited to join a local chorus. Dad chose the Bendix Male Chorus and often sang its solos.

Shown above are members of the Bendix Male Chorus as they appeared in a program May 3 at the Progress Club. The chorus, under the direction of Edward Soetje (extreme left first row), has just completed a most successful season climaxed by their brilliant performance in the annual state sing at Kokomo in April. Miss Betty Butler (extreme right first row) served as accompanist for the group. The members are planning a dinner party for their wives to be held in the near future.

The Bendix Male Chorus, 1945. Dad is in the first row, third from the left.
Source: *St. Joseph Herald Press, author's records.*

In the mid-1940s, Dad traveled to Nashville, Tennessee, where he cut a record and anticipated signing a recording contract. As the story goes, an agent offered Dad a contract, but my grandmother wanted him to stay on the farm, given that she had recently lost her husband and did not want to lose her only son as well. He acquiesced to his mother's wishes, declined the offer, and returned to Michigan. He kept the 78 rpm record, a melodic version of Schubert's Ave Maria. When I was a toddler, I accidentally broke the disk, and sadly, we lost the only known recording of his marvelous voice. Dad forever regretted, I believe, his decision to forego the contract and assume the relatively mundane life of a school teacher and administrator.

Dad and Mom spent three years in the Kalamazoo and Paw Paw area after their marriage in 1947 so that Dad could finish his undergraduate work at Western. Fourteen months later, I was born at Bronson Methodist Hospital in January 1949. The following spring, we moved to Buchanan, Michigan, a thriving, middle-class community of 5,000 people, where Dad taught 5th grade, and Mom, a newly-trained registered nurse, worked in the clinic associated with Clark Equipment, a manufacturer of excavators, forklifts, and other heavy equipment. Mom loved medicine and nursing and often worked weekends in the emergency room of the local hospital to earn extra money to support our family.

Mom enjoyed the proximity to her sister, my Aunt Carol, who ran Buchanan's A&W Drive-In each summer along with her husband, Bud. Uncle Bud, a coach and high school biology teacher, supplemented their income on summer weekends by working as a Berrien County Deputy Sheriff patrolling lakes and harbors. The two couples met frequently to drink beer and play poker, and in my youth, I looked forward eagerly to the visits to their drive-in, where Uncle Bud would treat me to a freshly grilled steak burger. On occasion, he even gave me a silver dollar, still used as legal tender in the early 1950s.

Having only one car, a maroon 1947 Buick convertible that my dad and mom had purchased on credit, Dad frequently drove Mom to the hospital when she worked Saturdays. Before leaving one Saturday morning, Dad added waste to our burn barrel, unaware that coals were still smoldering at its base. When Dad and I returned fifteen minutes later, the fire had spread to the dry grass of the vacant, half-acre lot next to our duplex. Although I found it thrilling when the fire trucks arrived in response to his frantic phone call, Dad did not, embarrassed by the commotion he had caused. Fortunately, the firemen extinguished the blaze quickly, averting any damage to our house, garage, and neighboring properties.

This was not Dad's only encounter with fire. When we moved to Three Oaks in 1953, his hot match set fire to scraps of plastic in the upstairs bathroom's wicker wastebasket. Rather than smother the flames with a towel, Dad attempted to carry the burning basket down the stairs and out the front door. When the flames reached his hand, he dropped the basket, and it bounced menacingly down the stairway. Fortunately, the only lasting damage was some burn marks on the Appalachian red oak steps and another blemish on Dad's ego.

Dad received a meager wage as an elementary school teacher, and to support our family, he took temporary jobs each summer. He often worked as a laborer, and while serving one summer as a carpenter's helper, an occupation to which he seemed genetically well-suited, he stepped on a large spike. The nail punctured the thin sole of his well-worn shoe and pierced his left foot, necessitating long hours of soaking his injured foot in Epsom salts. Thank goodness for Mom's skill as an ER nurse! After this experience, Dad concluded that becoming a salaried school administrator would be a far more satisfying and safer career than that of a struggling elementary school teacher who annually needed the supplemental income of summer employment.

In 1953, we left Buchanan and moved to Three Oaks, Michigan, a community of 1,200, where Dad became the elementary school principal. There, he wore many other hats, including those of a 5th grade teacher and the basketball coach of the 5th and 6th grade boys. As high school seniors, the team, composed of the players that Dad had recruited and coached in elementary school, achieved the #1 basketball ranking in Michigan's Class C, the state's designation for small-to-medium-sized high schools.

The talented Three Oaks Oakers barely missed the 1960 State Tournament when they lost the regional final in overtime to the Pete Gent-led Bangor team. Standing six feet, four inches tall, and towering over most of the Oakers, Gent would play basketball at Michigan State University and professional football as a wide receiver for the National Football League's Dallas Cowboys. Upon his retirement from football, the multi-talented Gent wrote *North Dallas Forty*, a novel based on his professional football experiences, as well as the screenplay for a movie of the same name, which starred Nick Nolte and Mac Davis.

In 1955, Dad became superintendent of the Three Oaks Schools at the remarkably young age of 32. His thin, prematurely gray hair, which gave him a distinguished appearance, made Dad seem older than his years. Because of the small size of the school district, Dad continued to serve many roles, including the treacherous task of scouting the back roads each winter to determine if the buses could run and the school could stay open. He installed steel chains on our aging Buick so that he could plow through deep snow drifts.

After one particularly snowy winter, the Buick's transmission failed from the demands of the chains and heavy snow. Undaunted, Dad purchased a new Buick Super with a big block Nailhead V8, named for the vertical, 'nails-in-a-plank'-like orientation of the engine's valves, so that he could drive through the deepest drifts. And how he needed the torque of the powerful V8. During one memorable snowstorm in the 1950s, nearly 48 inches of lake-effect snow fell in Three Oaks, a community located in west Michigan's snowbelt!

Dad loved to drive, especially in the spring, when he would visit Midwest colleges to recruit teachers for the school district. During one long road trip, he ran low on gas and coasted into a service station near South Bend, Indiana, to fill the Buick's tank. He was low on money, too, and only had his lucky coin, a 1923 silver dollar, to pay for the gas. Before completing the purchase, he confirmed that he could return later that week with a paper dollar to retrieve the coin. And he did just that. In Dad's day, a dollar could buy several gallons of gasoline. When I first started driving in the 1960s, I once paid 17 cents a gallon at a station on Plainfield Avenue north of Grand Rapids, Michigan.

In 1961, we moved from Three Oaks to Rockford, Michigan, where Dad assumed the position of superintendent of the Rockford Public Schools, a larger and more prestigious school district located thirteen miles north of Grand Rapids. Later, Dad enrolled in a doctoral program at Michigan State University in East Lansing, where he took classes in the summer. Dissatisfied with the quality and relevance of his education, he left the program before graduating. As was the case with a few other life choices, he regretted this decision, I believe, for his farewell words to me when I departed for college several years later were: "Don't stop until you get a doctorate."

Dad lived the adage 'if you can't say anything good, don't say anything'. I never heard him utter an unkind word about others, nor did I ever see or hear him argue with our mom. Although Dad was an introvert by nature, he also had a temper, and his mood could change abruptly, especially when my brother and I misbehaved. Dad, a perfectionist, had little tolerance for the flaws of others, including those of his own sons.

Superintendent, James Bale, at his desk, 1950s
Source: Unknown photographer

Dad had undoubtedly endured physical punishment from his father, who believed, like many parents of the day, that sparing the rod spoiled the child. Dad and Mom used similar disciplinary strategies when my brother and I were young. After moving to Rockford, Dad warned me as I entered junior high that if I got into trouble at school, I would get it 'double' at home. As the new superintendent of the Rockford Public Schools, Dad would not tolerate any embarrassment that a misbehaving son might bring to our family.

Midway through eighth grade, I misplaced my textbook on the day of a math quiz and quietly asked one of my classmates if I could look over at his book to see the problems. This arrangement worked well for the first ten minutes or so, until our teacher, Mr. Eby, noticed me peering at the book on the adjacent desk.

"Bale, where's your book?" he roared.

"I think I lost it, Mr. Eby."

"Go to the office . . . now! And don't come back until you find it."

I didn't argue with Mr. Eby, even though I knew that I would be in far greater trouble at home. So, I left the class and walked slowly down the long hallway to the principal's office. I explained to the secretary why I was there, and she looked up briefly, pointed to a chair, and curtly said, "Take a seat."

The uncomfortable hardwood chair upon which I sat happened to be next to the large wood bin that served as the school's lost and found department. There, right on the very top, was my book. The secretary looked up again but didn't respond when I sighed and then laughed. While I couldn't return to Mr. Eby's room for the remainder of that hour, finding my book enabled me to rejoin the class the next day and relieved me of any harsh punishment at home. I often wondered if a mischievous classmate had 'lost' it for me, hoping to learn how my dad would react. Being the superintendent's son was never easy.

Whenever I misbehaved, which was fortunately infrequent, I got the belt until I was nearly 14 years old. By then, I had grown big enough to resist Dad, although I never fought back. But it wasn't his concern for my size or strength that finally made Dad stop. Although I've forgotten what provoked his anger that day, I do remember how our interaction ended. After the third blow from the belt, I shouted through my tears, "Dad, it wasn't me." He stopped, said nothing, and quietly walked upstairs. He never used the belt on me again.

Even before he retired, Dad would drive the 70 miles from Rockford to The Maples each summer weekend to mow the farm's two acres of lush grass. I often wondered if the sweet aroma of the newly-mown lawn rekindled pleasant memories of his childhood. Wearing a straw hat and smoking a pipe, Dad would ride his aging Snapper mower and cut the tall grass in ever-expanding swaths until he finished the last bit of lawn. He would then sit for a spell to admire his work, talk briefly with his mother, and when they had finished their conversation, he would return to Rockford.

The tobacco-filled pipe eventually became his downfall. First, leukoplakia, precancerous lesions of his mouth and gums, appeared, and later, advanced atherosclerotic disease of his coronary arteries caused by his smoking led to his first heart attack at the age of 57. I'm certain that the attack, which he initially ignored, occurred while he was deer hunting with friends in northern Michigan. Emergency coronary artery bypass surgery would be needed to save his life. He required a second surgery in the early 1990s and succumbed to heart failure in 1997 at the age of 74.

When Aunt Claribel died in 1983, my wife and I needed to drive the 330 miles from Iowa City, where we had moved in 1982, to Paw Paw to attend her funeral. Martha, our four-year-old son, Zach, and I awoke before dawn the day of her funeral, packed our car, and headed east on I-80. We had driven less than 30 miles in pitch darkness when we encountered dense fog so thick that we could barely see the white lines of the expressway. Head lights would occasionally appear behind us, bobbing specter-like in the gloom, and massive semi-trucks, undaunted by the poor visibility, would sail past.

"This is insane," Martha had said, pleading that we should return to Iowa City. "We could get killed."

Even though I knew that she was probably right, we did not stop. Dad needed me, but at the time, I didn't fully understand how much.

7

Mom, I-94, and The Great Recession

As time passed, I realized that I also needed to know more about my mother, the person who told the lie, and her ancestors. Would I discover information about her life and family that would help explain her actions? Would I eventually learn why my mom had never asked my dad, her husband of 49 years, how his father died?

My mom was born in Albion, Michigan, a working-class community in south-central Michigan, approximately 90 miles west of Detroit. At the time of my mom's birth in 1925, Albion was a thriving factory town with a population of approximately 8,000. Settled in 1835 and incorporated as a village in 1855, Albion sits near the eastern end of Michigan's I-94 corridor, a 275-mile expanse that begins at New Buffalo on Lake Michigan on the west side of the state and ends on the east side at Port Huron, near the southern tip of Lake Huron. In between lie the cities of Benton Harbor, St. Joseph, Kalamazoo, Battle Creek, Marshall, Albion, Jackson, Ann Arbor, Ypsilanti, and Detroit, as well as numerous towns and villages, including Paw Paw, Lawton, and Mattawan.

I-94, a major route in the interstate highway system, materialized when Congress enacted the Federal Aid Highway Act of 1956, and

President Dwight D. Eisenhower signed the bill into law on June 29th of the same year. Congress and the President believed that we needed a national highway system that would facilitate the transport of mobile missiles in the event of a war with Russia. The Cold War had begun, and the leaders of the U.S. military worried that the Russians would strike first and destroy our nation's fixed installations of intercontinental ballistic missiles, the ICBMs. Interstate highways, such as I-94, would serve important strategic purposes.

Interstate highway bridge over the Mississippi River, present day
Source: The author

Although construction of I-94 officially started in 1958 with a 12-mile stretch of divided, limited-access highway near Jamestown, North Dakota, I-94 actually originated in Michigan as a result of the state's pivotal role in World War II. With the U.S. anticipating that we would join the war against Germany, the Michigan State Highway Department built the Willow Run Expressway in 1941 to bring workers and materials to the new Ford Motor Company bomber factory near Ypsilanti, 40 miles west of Detroit. There, the state's engineers designed specialized ramps so that workers could enter and exit the parking lots of the factory directly from the expressway.

More than 40,000 people would eventually work at the enormous plant. Many of the early employees were women, and by 1943, women comprised nearly two-thirds of the aviation workforce nationwide. Although the true identity of the legendary Rosie the Riveter was a source of debate and competition among the supervisors of the WWII bomber plants, many authorities currently believe that she was Rosie Will Monroe, a riveter at the Willow Run factory. Had my mom not been a high school sophomore when the war began, she might have joined Rosie and her coworkers in building the B-24 Liberator bomber.

Until the B-24 appeared, the B-17 Flying Fortress, designed and built by the Boeing Aircraft Company, Seattle, Washington, had been the preferred long-range bomber of the U.S. Army Air Corps, the forerunner of the U.S. Air Force. Like the B-17, four massive 1200 horsepower engines powered the B-24, but unlike the B-17, the B-24 had two vertical tail stabilizers and a Davis wing, a unique engineering design that reduced the plane's drag and improved its fuel efficiency. With these innovations, the B-24 had a longer range, a larger payload, and a higher top speed than the B-17.

When the U.S. government invited Consolidated Aircraft Corporation of San Diego, California, to compete for bomber production and design a replacement for the B-17, the Army Air Corps specified that the new bomber should be capable of flying at 35,000 feet and have a range of 3,000 miles. While the B-24 production models did not fully meet these requirements, with a ceiling of 34,000 feet and a combat range of 2800 miles, the B-24's overall performance convinced the federal government to award the design contract to Consolidated.

More than 18,000 B-24s were built during World War II, according to the Aviation History Online Museum, and they dropped more than 630,000 tons of bombs during their deployment. At their peak, the workers of the massive Willow Run factory, supported by sister factories in Oklahoma and Texas, could complete the final assembly of a B-24 bomber in an astonishing 63 minutes! April 1944 saw the factory finish

428 bombers in just a single month. By contrast, assembling a new Ford F-150, currently the best-selling pickup truck in the U.S., takes 20 hours, even with the help of robots. As for B-24 production, the Willow Run plant led the way, building nearly 50% of the entire fleet.

The Willow Run Expressway, which would eventually become part of I-94, later connected with the Detroit Industrial Expressway to the east, and by the time the war ended in 1945, motorists could travel from midtown Detroit to Ypsilanti on a high-speed, limited-access freeway. Construction of I-94 continued in the 1950s westward toward Lake Michigan. By 1960, the work crews had completed I-94 from Detroit on the east to New Buffalo, a lakeside community at the Michigan-Indiana border seven miles west of my childhood home of Three Oaks.

For a brief period, Michigan considered naming the new highway M 112 as a historical tribute to US 12, the expressway's predecessor. But the state reconsidered and replaced the 'M' designation with an 'I' to ensure that Michigan would benefit from the federal funds being awarded to states for their participation in the interstate highway system. When I-94 reached Mattawan, four miles east of Bale's corners, the expressway's route paralleled US 12, Red Arrow Highway, less than one mile south of The Maples. To our family's good fortune, the new expressway did not divide the Bale property as it had with many other nearby farms, passing just yards away.

Because of resistance from the State of Indiana, construction of I-94's final short segment, intended to connect Michigan's I-94 with Indiana's I-80, the Indiana Toll Road, took several years to complete. Concerned that connecting I-80 with I-94 would divert traffic from the lucrative Indiana Toll Road to Michigan's toll-free I-94, the State of Indiana withheld the construction permits until the late 1960s. After considerable political wrangling, the construction crews finally built the I-94 to I-80 interchange, and in 1972, the entire Michigan segment of I-94 opened.

Construction on I-94 did not end then, however. Because steel had been diverted to the war effort in 1941, steel mesh did not reinforce the concrete of the Willow Run section. Consequently, the pavement deteriorated more rapidly than expected. In the same summer that I-94's west end successfully connected with I-80, construction resumed on I-94's east end. This marked the beginning of summer road construction, the bane of all who drive the interstate highway system.

Living in southwest Michigan, my family had eagerly anticipated the completion of I-94 and the convenience and safety it would provide. Having a divided, limited-access highway meant that we could avoid the hazardous two-lane highways, such as M-60, that characterized Michigan's highway system in the 1950s and early 1960s. We would eventually spend countless hours on I-94 and its sister highway, I-96, driving to and from Grand Rapids, Albion, and Paw Paw to visit our relatives. And after graduating from high school, I frequently traveled Michigan's interstate highways while attending the University of Michigan in Ann Arbor.

Driving I-94 today provides a rich panorama of Michigan's Lower Peninsula. The journey from West Michigan begins with the sister cities of Benton Harbor and St. Joseph, which border Lake Michigan at the far western end of the I-94 corridor. While only the St. Joseph River, spanned by two short bridges, separates the two cities, the communities are worlds apart.

Benton Harbor, named for Thomas Hart Benton, the Missouri Senator who championed Michigan's entry into the Union in 1837, currently has a population of nearly 9,000. Of these, 87% are Black, and less than 10% are white. Benton Harbor's per capita and median household incomes, ~$18,000 and ~$27,000 in 2022, are among Michigan's lowest and far below the national figures of ~$65,000 and ~$75,000. Nearly 45% of Benton Harbor's residents live below the poverty line, and less than 10% of adults in the city have a college education. As of 2022, 35% of Benton Harbor's adult population was unemployed.

St. Joseph, named for the adjacent St. Joseph River, has a similar population, approximately 8,000, but in striking contrast to Benton Harbor, nearly 90% of its citizens are white and only 4% are Black. The per capita income, ~$55,000, and the median household income,

~$79,000, are considerably higher than those of Benton Harbor. More than 50% of the adults in St. Joseph have a college education, and only ~9% of the city's inhabitants live in poverty. The city's unemployment rate averages 4.5%, far lower than Benton Harbor's.

Why are these adjacent cities of nearly equal size so vastly different? History suggests that systemic racism underlies, at least in part, this tragic tale of two cities. In the 1950s and 1960s, well-paying jobs lured southern Blacks to Benton Harbor, and they prospered. But when the factories later closed and companies left Benton Harbor as a result of industrial globalization, the unemployed population grew rapidly. The city's white citizens left Benton Harbor, and by the late 1980s, dramatic differences in demographics, education, and income had emerged.

Benton Harbor suffers from the effects of white flight, a term coined in the 1950s to describe the exodus of whites from cities to the suburbs. In this instance, the more mobile whites left Benton Harbor for employment in nearby St. Joseph and other, predominantly-white West Michigan communities. The Blacks, who lacked similar opportunities, remained in Benton Harbor and struggled.

Kalamazoo, the next city on our eastward journey, houses two excellent institutions of higher education: Kalamazoo College, a small, private liberal arts college, and Western Michigan University, a medium-sized state university. Founded in 1833, four years before Michigan achieved statehood, Kalamazoo College, better known as 'K College', ranks in the top 100 of the more than 500 liberal arts colleges in the U.S.; its tuition and fees approach $55,000 annually, making K College an expensive place to obtain a college education. But the money can be well spent. Loren Pope, the former education editor of the New York Times and author of the highly-acclaimed book *Colleges that Change Lives*, consistently listed K College as one of the top 40 U.S. liberal arts colleges.

Although considerably larger, with approximately 22,000 students, but far less expensive, Western Michigan University (WMU), known simply as 'Western', can also change lives. My grandmother received her teacher's certificate from Western States Normal School, the university's forerunner, and Dad received his bachelor's degree from WMU in the late 1940s. Moreover, WMU now houses the Bronson Nursing School, which Mom attended when it was the Bronson Methodist Hospital School of Nursing. Without Dad's education at Western, Mom's training at Bronson, and the chance encounter in Kalamazoo that led to their romance and marriage, neither my brother nor I would exist.

In an altruistic effort to improve Kalamazoo's future, wealthy, anonymous donors created the Kalamazoo Promise, a fund that provides up to 100% of the costs of college tuition and fees to the graduates of Kalamazoo's public schools. The donors hope to remove the economic barriers that prevent many high school graduates, especially those from low-income families, from obtaining a college education. Since its inauguration in 2005, the Kalamazoo Promise has funded the education of hundreds of students, and similar programs have appeared in nearly a dozen U.S. communities.

Traveling east on I-94, we next reach Battle Creek, a city of 51,000 about 30 miles from Kalamazoo. Although its name, Battle Creek, implies that a major conflict led to the city's moniker, the 'battle' was only a minor altercation between Native Potawatomi Indians and a federal surveyor in the early 1800s. Battle Creek is best known as 'The Cereal City', a nickname that honors the extraordinary contributions of Kellogg and Post, the giants of a cereal industry that originated in Battle Creek in the late 1800s. At one time, Battle Creek had more than 100 cereal companies! Today, Kellogg's and Post are household names for nearly all Americans.

Just past the midpoint of the I-94 corridor lies Jackson, Michigan, a city of approximately 34,000. Jackson once housed the largest walled prison in the world, Jackson State Prison. Also known as the Michigan State Prison, the prison served the entire state for nearly one hundred years, and within its walls, the prison contained farmland, factories, and numerous cell blocks.

When the prison closed in 1934, a portion of the imposing structure became the State of Michigan's surplus equipment store. I accompanied my dad there several times in the 1950s and 1960s, when he purchased items for the Three Oaks and Rockford school systems. Standing next to the prison's massive stone walls had a chilling effect. I often sensed that the ghosts of former inmates would suddenly appear and extract their revenge. Fortunately, I always escaped unscathed.

Jackson sits amidst the Irish Hills, vestiges of the most recent North American glacial period, the Wisconsin Glaciation. During a protracted ice age that lasted for more than 50,000 years, massive glaciers covered New England; New York; most of Canada; nearly all of Wisconsin, North Dakota, and Minnesota; parts of Illinois, Indiana, Iowa, and South Dakota; and the entire state of Michigan. When the glaciers receded 11,000 years ago, their lateral and terminal moraines formed the Irish Hills, and their melting ice created numerous freshwater lakes that now dot the landscape of Michigan's Lower Peninsula.

The rolling terrain and pristine lakes of the Jackson area fostered the development of several tourist attractions along US 12, as well as more than a few tourist traps, in the 1920s, 1950s, and 1970s. Such attractions included Frontier City, Mystery Hill, Prehistoric Forest, and Stagecoach Stop, USA. For adventurous Michiganders who could not travel to the Smoky or Rocky Mountains, visiting the Irish Hills could satisfy, at least in part, the urge to explore.

To the west of Jackson lies Marshall, Michigan, a tranquil community noted for its exceptional architecture. Each year, the Marshall Historical Society hosts tours that enable visitors to stroll through the town's picturesque homes and unique commercial buildings dating from the 1840s. As with Albion and nearby Concord, the Kalamazoo River served as the focal point for the settlement of the village of Marshall. Saw and grist mills, constructed in the 1830s, capitalized on the abundant water power, and farmers found the fertile land bordering the Kalamazoo River and its tributary, Rice Creek, conducive to growing corn and other grains.

Their location on the principal stagecoach route and later, the major rail line between Detroit and Chicago, brought a steady stream of settlers, including my mother's ancestors, to Marshall, Albion, and nearby communities. The completion of the Erie Canal in 1825 further accelerated the westward migration of people into Michigan. Michigan's white population grew exponentially from just under 4,000 in 1800 to nearly 175,000 when the Michigan Territory became the 26th U.S. state in 1837.

Native peoples, especially the Potawatomi, had inhabited the Kalamazoo River valley, including the future sites of Jackson, Marshall, and Albion, for centuries. The rapid influx of settlers into the homelands of the native people, which had an estimated population of only 2,000 to 4,000, led to numerous conflicts in the early 1800s. As recorded by Ken Wyatt of the Jackson Citizen Patriot, the 4th U.S. Infantry and 2nd U.S. Cavalry, under the command of Brig. Gen. Hugh Brady, came to Jackson "to gather up the Indians."

Empowered by the Treaty of 1833, a biased document that favored the white settlers, the soldiers systematically removed approximately 1,500 Potawatomi men, women, and children from southeast Michigan and marched them to Detroit, where they were transported unceremoniously by boat to a reservation near Green Bay, Wisconsin. Today, remnants of the Potawatomi Nation persist in the reservations of the Nottawaseppi Huron and Pokagon Bands in West Michigan and the Hannahville Potawatomi in Michigan's Upper Peninsula.

My mom, the first child of Everett and Vera, my maternal grandparents, grew up in a small house on Eaton Street on the north side of Albion, approximately 90 years after the soldiers dispersed the Potawatomi Nation. Vera had apparently inherited the property from her family. Mom had a single sister, Carol, who was four years younger. With Mom's passing in 2015, one month after her 90th birthday, the opportunity to obtain additional oral history about her family vanished, and I must rely on my memory, as well as a few photos, to recreate their life story.

The earliest picture I have of my mom shows her picking tulips in her father's garden at 3 years of age. She loved to tend his garden, but not until her retirement did she have sufficient time and resources to plant her own. In the 1950s, she once attempted to grow vegetables in the backyard of our Three Oaks home, but her efforts failed miserably when I pulled and discarded all of the young tomato plants while weeding her garden. She lacked the money and the will to replace them.

Although only a young child in 1929, Mom, like my dad, remembered the Depression as a time of intense sadness. Her father, a factory worker, labored tirelessly to provide for his family, but he received low wages and constantly faced the threat of layoffs. I do not know if he lost his job, like so many others, when the Great Depression struck and deepened. Mom's childhood in Albion must have been difficult, at best. She once told me that luxury in her household consisted of a loaf of freshly baked bread and a gallon of whole milk, from which they would skim the cream to make butter. Like many Albion families of the Depression era, they raised chickens for meat and eggs and grew carrots, tomatoes, potatoes, and corn in a family garden that occupied much of their backyard.

My mom, age 3, picking flowers in her father's
garden
Source: Unknown photographer

My maternal grandfather's work at an Albion foundry brought not only the risk of layoffs but also the danger of disabling injuries. He never told me about the excruciating industrial accident that led to the loss of his eye, and sadly, I never asked him about it. After recovering, he was left with a glass eye, which he removed from its socket each evening and placed in an eye cup filled with distilled water. I sensed that Mom was often embarrassed by her father, an unskilled laborer with an 8th grade education. She rarely discussed his background and never discussed the accident or his work at the foundry.

One of Grandfather's eye cups
Source: The author

At one time, Albion had five busy foundries, and the largest of these, Union Steel Products, employed more than 1,000 people. Originally founded in 1902 as the Union Steel Screen Company, Union Steel moved to Albion in 1905, where the name was changed to Union Steel Products in 1915. In its heyday, Union Steel was the world's largest manufacturer of oven and broiler pan shelves, as well as many types of wire baskets.

While the foundries provided steady work for Albion's men and women, they seemed like accidents waiting to happen. Day in and day out, foundry workers, like my grandfather, poured molten metal, hot enough to boil blood or fry skin, into molds for iron, steel, and aluminum, creating scores of parts for cars, trucks, airplanes, and all kinds of machinery. At the time, the U.S. was the epicenter of the world's iron and steel industry. In the early 1960s, I often traveled with my family through Gary, Indiana, the location of numerous active blast furnaces and massive steel mills, and we needed to close the car windows tightly to escape the pervasive soot and obnoxious odors.

My maternal grandfather at Pilgrim Manor,
Grand Rapids, Michigan, in the 1980s
Source: The author

Mom's school pictures show a serious, bespectacled student with red hair and freckles. She told me that her elementary school classmates often called her 'four eyes' or 'freckle face' in malicious behaviors that we would now call bullying. Such teasing makes one stronger, she used to say, although a degree of sadness and insecurity always seemed to underlie Mom's confident veneer. She was a stubborn child, or so she said, not always acquiescing to the demands of her teachers or her stern Germanic mother, who worked at home as a seamstress. Mom had a temper, too, and occasionally reminded my brother and me not to repeat her 'French'.

Mom performed well in school, receiving A's and a few B's; she loved science and dreamt of becoming a nurse. To my knowledge, she did not participate in sports or other extracurricular activities, choosing instead to spend her free time reading good books or studying for exams. I suspect that she was a 'front row sitter', eager to raise her hand and ask questions whenever the opportunity arose. She might have dreamed of being a doctor, too, had this career path been available to young women in the 1940s.

Upon graduating from high school in 1943, Mom was accepted into the three-year nursing program at Bronson Methodist Hospital in Kalamazoo, Michigan. She loved nursing, despite the rigors of the classwork and the long hours in the emergency room or on the hospital wards. She experienced firsthand the hierarchy of medicine, quickly learning that a nurse always did what the doctor ordered.

The nursing students of her day, almost all women in their late teens or early twenties, revered the doctors, all men, who visited Bronson and lectured on topics such as orthopedics, neurology, and cardiology. Whenever the doctors entered the lecture hall, the nursing students were expected to stand until the doctors reached the lectern and began to speak. When the doctors finished their lectures, the nursing students stood once again and remained standing until the doctors exited the room. No wonder Mom and her classmates hoped that their own children would become doctors.

When Mom left Albion for nursing school in Kalamazoo, approximately 50 miles west on US 12, she vowed that she would never return. Although Albion's civic and college leaders tried to encourage communication and cooperation, tension persisted between the townspeople and Albion College, a well-respected liberal arts school on Albion's east side. The factory workers and their families, the 'townies', disliked the aloof intellectuals, and the college faculty and students, the 'gownies', apparently had limited respect for the workers. Mom felt trapped in the middle. She enjoyed intellectual pursuits and considered becoming a writer. But she also loved her father, despite his simple life and eighth-grade education, and supported him unconditionally.

Racial tensions existed in Albion as well, during and after the years that Mom lived at home. Fortunately, Albion did not witness any violence in the summer of 1967, the year of the destructive Detroit race riot, a tragic event during which 43 people died. Mom's own subliminal racism would occasionally surface when she talked about going to the 'other side of the tracks', where the Blacks lived, or to 'honky town', where the Poles lived. Mom had many reasons to seek opportunities elsewhere.

My mom and her parents sat silently during the hour-long drive to Kalamazoo for her matriculation into nursing school. The stress of

leaving her family and home town became palpable somewhere between Battle Creek and Kalamazoo when their aging automobile broke
down, and it slowed to a stop on the highway shoulder.

When her father suggested that maybe she shouldn't go to nursing
school after all, Mom replied, "I'm going to get there, even if I have
to walk."

My mom, circa 1950s
Source: Unknown photographer

Mom received a three-year
R.N. degree from Bronson in 1947.
She often considered returning to
school to obtain a B.S.-R.N., since
the extra year of education would
add credibility to her nursing
degree. But marriage, work, and
young children got in her way,
and she never had the time or
the resources to return to college.
She spent most of her final years
of nursing, which spanned nearly
five decades, employed in the office of thoracic surgeons in Grand
Rapids, Michigan. After Dad retired in the 1980s and they win-
tered in Florida to escape the cold
and snow, Mom would return to
their Michigan home each summer to work in the surgeons' office.
There, she ran circles around the younger nurses, even into her 70s.
Mom always arrived early and stayed late, never leaving until she was
confident that she had met all of the needs of her patients. My father's
words encouraged me to seek a doctorate, but my mother's actions
inspired me to become a physician.

By the time the Great Recession hit Michigan in 2007, Mom had retired
and settled into her new home at The Maples. Living there with Job,
Mom subsisted on her monthly Social Security checks and the meager

amount of money she received from leasing the farmland. When Dad retired and began receiving a pension from the State of Michigan, he made the ill-advised decision to waive the spousal benefit that would have provided income for my mom after his death. When he died in 1997, Mom was on her own.

The Michiganders who lived along I-94, both farmers and city dwellers alike, struggled during the dreadful economic conditions of the Great Recession. When General Motors filed for Chapter 11 bankruptcy protection in 2009, unemployment surged throughout Michigan, and by September of that year, it had exceeded 15% statewide. In some west Michigan communities, such as Holland, a picturesque lakeside resort town approximately 50 miles north of Benton Harbor, as many as 25% of the adults lacked work during the Recession. At the height of the Great Recession, approximately 700,000 Michiganders were unemployed, reflecting the catastrophic loss of more than 300,000 well-paying jobs in the automobile and related industries. In 2009, Michigan became the only state to experience declines in both birthrate and population.

Just as they did during the Great Depression, rates of mental illness and suicide soared during the 2007-2009 recession, paralleling the dramatic rise in unemployment. The overall rate of suicide in the U.S. rose by almost 5%, and nearly 5,000 suicides can be attributed nationwide to the economic miseries of the Great Recession. Among the most vulnerable were young adults, ethnic or racial minorities, and women.

The same qualities that enabled Mom to leave her family and survive nursing school sustained her during the dark days of the Recession. She lived frugally at the farm, clipping coupons and shopping the sales at the stores in Kalamazoo and Paw Paw. For years, Mom had purchased her clothes and shoes during the annual sales at Jacobson's and Herpolsheimer's department stores in Grand Rapids, even when she and Dad had steady incomes from nursing and education administration. She took immense pride in her ability to dress well at half the cost.

While growing up in Three Oaks and Rockford, I never appreciated how carefully Mom managed our family's finances. Her medical background taught her how to inspect food for spoilage, and she often bought outdated bread and canned goods, which she fed to us with impunity. When my brother and I were young, she would take us to the local orchards, including those of the Andersons, to help her pick up the 'drops', the apples that had fallen from the trees. Mom could buy these for just pennies a pound. She would then spend weekends canning applesauce, which our family would eat during the long Michigan winters.

Mom's memories of the Great Depression continued to influence her actions throughout her life and enabled her to survive the Great Recession without incurring additional debt. Undoubtedly affected by the sad stories of families who did not survive the Depression, Mom admonished my brother and me to never buy food on credit, and to this day, I rarely have. Even buying food with a debit card makes me pause to consider the consequences.

Mom never complained about her life during the Great Recession. She used to tell me that she had her cat, the farm, and her friends. What more did she need? She rarely ate out, and when she did, she went to Subway, the quaint little sandwich shop she had discovered in Paw Paw. Mom always lived life with childlike wonder, even into her 80s.

Throughout my childhood, Mom told me that her father's ancestors came from Sweden as part of the mass migration from Northern Europe that began in the 1840s and peaked around 1900. Nearly 10% of the Swedish populace immigrated to the U.S. during those years. Because of her story, I grew up believing that I was 25% Swedish. When selected by the Rockford Rotary Club in 1966 to be a summer exchange student with Youth for Understanding, an organization founded two decades earlier by Rachel Andresen, I naturally chose to live in Sweden.

My summer in Sweden was immensely satisfying, concordant with my blond hair, reddish-blonde beard, and presumed genetic heritage. I lived with a wonderful family in Ekenässjön, a tiny village in central Småland, and spent a glorious summer eating delicious Swedish food, fishing for pike or perch in the Baltic Sea, and traveling in Sweden and Norway during the nationwide July holiday. I felt at home, especially when hiking in the birch and spruce forests of Scandinavia or walking the rocky shoreline of the Baltic Sea.

When my wife and I traveled to Sweden in 1994 for a scientific meeting, I searched the Stockholm phonebook for potential relatives and found no one with my maternal grandfather's surname. Upon our return home later that summer, I recounted this experience to my mother, and her defensive response was a curt "Well, maybe they're British." Having lived for years believing and broadcasting to others that I had Swedish roots, I was stunned. Had Mom told me another lie?

To help soothe the wound and satisfy my growing curiosity, I eventually sent a saliva sample for genetic testing. The analysis indicated that my origins are entirely Northern European, 75% English or Welsh, with the remainder a mix of German and Scandinavian, especially Norwegian. So, I do have some Scandinavian blood after all! Was it possible that my ancestors invaded the British Isles with other Vikings and settled there, becoming farmers and sheepherders?

Stockholm, Sweden, Old Town, 2019
Source: *The author*

8

⁘

Taylor the Tailor

Given Mom's misleading information about my Swedish ancestry, I was more than a bit skeptical when she started to tell me about our ancestors in Concord, Michigan, and their participation in the Underground Railroad. But in contrast to many of her stories, Mom had tangible proof this time. In her lap, she held a faded black-and-white photograph showing a house, a horse, two cows, and some people. As we sat together in her country kitchen, she told me the story of how our family helped runaway slaves escape to Canada.

"This is the Taylor-Reynold's farm in Concord, Michigan," she began. "The farm sat at the top of a hill overlooking the millpond of the Kalamazoo River. My grandmother, Mary Elizabeth Reynolds, was born here. The picture shows her parents standing in front of the house. Her father, my great-grandfather, holds the reins of their horse near the front porch, and my great-grandmother stands next to the large tree on the other side of the yard."

"This home," she continued, "was part of the Underground Railroad. Runaway slaves would come up the Kalamazoo River at night, and when they reached Concord, a tiny village of less than 500 people, my great-grandparents would hide the slaves in a secret closet in the house."

Concord and several other villages in Jackson County, Michigan, I would later learn, had been critical waypoints in the runaway slaves' journey to freedom.

The Taylor-Reynolds home, Concord, Michigan, date unknown
Source: Unknown photographer

Described by many historians as a 'peculiar institution', slavery began in the New World during the colonial period, initially in Brazil and the Caribbean and subsequently in the American colonies. Several factors contributed to slavery's appearance in the New World. Foremost among them was the New World's rapidly expanding agrarian economy. Benefiting from the fertile soils and favorable climate, numerous landowners established immense plantations throughout the region. Plantations in Brazil and the Caribbean Islands produced sugarcane, while those in Virginia and Maryland grew and exported tobacco. Later, cotton plantations arose throughout the Deep South. Planting and harvesting each of these crops required a sizeable workforce that would toil for hours in hot and humid conditions.

The second and more critical factor in the emergence of slavery was the willingness of America's founders to condone forced labor. The first slaves arrived in the American colonies from Africa in 1619. Soon thereafter, slavery spread rapidly throughout the colonies, becoming legal in all, even in those that would later become abolitionist states. According to Peter Kolchin, who wrote extensively about the history of slavery in America, two-thirds of the first dozen presidents of the United States owned slaves. George Washington and Thomas Jefferson each owned nearly two hundred slaves, although the majority of Washington's slaves were apparently the property of his wife, Martha.

A cotton field in the South, present day
Source: The author

Perhaps the only practice comparable to New World slavery in the 1600s was Russian serfdom, another form of coerced labor that supported an agrarian economy. And as was the case with slavery, serfdom also enhanced the wealth of the landowners. Like the slaves in America, Russian serfs obsequiously served their masters, but in contrast to American slaves, serfs experienced far greater independence. Russian society accorded the serfs, also known as the peasants, certain rights and privileges, such as the ability to own land, marry, and form communities, that America did not bestow upon its slaves. Over time, Russian society accepted the peasants, albeit at the lowest tier of its social hierarchy, but by virtue of their skin color and African origins, the slaves in America remained outcasts.

Indentured servitude, another labor practice in the New World, resembled slavery in the master's absolute control of the servant. And like a slave, an indentured servant could be sold as property and undergo harsh corporal punishment whenever he or she disobeyed. That said, indentured servitude also differed from slavery in several fundamental ways. First and foremost, indentured servants typically entered the arrangement voluntarily, often using servitude as a means to gain passage across the Atlantic Ocean. As many as three-quarters of the English immigrants who came to America in the mid-1600s arrived as indentured servants, indebted to their masters for the cost of the transatlantic journey. The manifest of the Mary Catherine, the ship that brought the Taylors, my ancestors, to America from England in the early 1800s, listed two passengers as servants, suggesting that they were indentured to other travelers. Most importantly, indentured servitude had explicit time limits. Indentured men or women served for fixed periods of four or five years, although their masters could force children to work for seven or more years.

In contrast to slaves, servants would typically be compensated for their service upon completion of their indenture, and the compensation, known as freedom dues, could be prearranged at the time of indenture. Some might be granted 25 to 50 acres of land on the western frontier, a practice that helped expand the size of the American colonies. Others might receive tangible goods. Pennsylvania law of 1700, as one example, required that each man who completed four or more years of servitude "shall be clothed with two complete suits of apparel, whereof one shall be new, and shall be also furnished with one axe, one grubbing hoe, and one weeding hoe." Freedmen or women could receive money or a horse in lieu of clothing.

Some statutes describing the compensation for those who completed their indenture now seem almost humorous in their detail. A 1715 Maryland law, later known as 'Bacon's Law,' specified that a suit of apparel for former servants consisted of "1 new hat; 1 good suit (coat and breeches) . . . 1 new shirt of white linen; 1 pair of shoes and stockings" for men, and "a Waist Coat or Petticoat of new half-thick or Pennistone (*a heavy woolen fabric*); a new shift of white linen (two suits); shoes and stockings; a blue apron and two Caps of white linen" for women.

In large measure, indenturing arose from the economic necessities of two groups of people: the impoverished people of the British Isles who needed to leave their countries to find employment, and the land owners of colonial America who wanted an inexpensive labor force to work in their fields or households. Sometimes known as white servitude, indentured servitude in the New World likely evolved from the apprenticeship system, a form of free or low-wage labor that had existed in Europe for centuries. Colonial statutes, such as the Virginia Charter of 1618, institutionalized indenturing through the 'headright', a process by which land owners would receive fifty acres for each person they brought from England. According to Anna Suranyi, who summarized indenturing in the Oxford Research Encyclopedia of American History, some 300,000 people made their way to America through indentured servitude.

For more than two hundred years, slavery flourished in the Americas, and over those two centuries, slave traders, primarily originating in England, transported more than 12,000,000 African men, women, and children to the New World. Although the majority of slave ships brought slaves to Brazil and the Caribbean Islands of Cuba, Haiti, and Puerto Rico, slave traders delivered approximately one million Africans to the U.S. prior to 1808, when Congress banned the importation of slaves. Africans entered slavery through numerous demeaning pathways: as prisoners of war sold to slave traders by the victors; as criminals or debtors; and, worst of all, as the victims of kidnapping. And as noted by Kolchin, "slaves destined for America lost everything they knew . . . home, possessions, loved ones."

The Africans brought to America on slave ships endured deplorable conditions during the long ocean voyage. Bound with chains and packed together like animals, the slaves traveled in dark, crowded cargo holds and faced torture, disease, dehydration, and starvation. Numerous slaves died en route; as many as 2 million African slaves did not complete the transatlantic crossing. Some slave traders actually threw their captives overboard to lighten a ship's load or benefit from insurance payments for 'lost' cargo. And an unknown number of slaves bound for America chose suicide at sea as a means to end their suffering.

Unlike my white ancestors, black slaves did not rejoice when they reached the New World. Upon their arrival in America, African slaves would be tethered, placed in holding pens, much as one might keep sheep or cattle, and sold at auction to the highest bidders. Some slaves would work as domestics in the homes of northern or southern gentry, but many more labored in the fields of the southern plantations. There, the slaves experienced inhumane treatment that could include overcrowding, malnutrition, and unimaginable punishment, particularly when slaves defied their masters or attempted to escape. Southern masters often whipped unruly slaves to keep them in line. With little fear of retaliation, the most mean-spirited of the overseers tortured slaves unmercifully, resorting to branding, mutilation, public hanging, or even the castration of male slaves.

The Alabama River, near Montgomery, a waterway frequently used by slavers to transport and distribute African slaves
Source: The author

James David Taylor, my maternal great-great grandfather, was born in Macclesfield, England, to John and Martha Taylor in 1810. Located in Cheshire County, Macclesfield dates from the 12th century, when King Edward I granted the town's first charter. The community prospered, and by 1830, Macclesfield's numerous silk mills employed more than 10,000 people, making the town the world's largest producer of finished silk. In 1832, James married Rachel Seech, and on their honeymoon, the newlyweds left their English family and friends and traveled from Liverpool to New York on the barque Mary Catherine. The Taylors arrived at Ellis Island on July 9, 1832, and like the Bales, who would arrive in America on their honeymoon almost two decades later, the Taylors never returned to England.

The Taylor's crossing of the Atlantic took nearly 50 days. The passenger manifest, compiled by Master John Carr, the ship's captain, upon the arrival of the Mary Catherine in New York, shows that the vessel, a three-masted clipper ship, brought 140 passengers to America. Of these, 28, including the Taylors, traveled in the second cabin, whereas the remainder sailed in steerage. The Mary Catherine's manifest contained no record of any first-cabin, i.e., first-class, passengers.

In stark contrast to the kidnapped African slaves, the Taylors and the other passengers in second cabin, also known as the intermediates, benefited from comfortable accommodations and wholesome foods prepared and served by the ship's cook and stewards. In the early vessels, the second cabin passengers traveled in private staterooms containing two narrow berths, one above the other, and a tiny closet. The space between the berths and the closet, although cramped, had sufficient room for a wooden stool or chair upon which a passenger could sit while dressing or reading. Even the passengers in steerage on the Mary Catherine traveled in relative comfort when compared with those on board the slave ships.

Although the four handwritten pages of the Mary Catherine's manifest contained limited information about its passengers (only their name, age, occupation, country of origin, and destination), the manifest nonetheless provides a useful snapshot of the people who emigrated from Europe to the U.S. in the 1830s. From this, I learned that young men comprised approximately one-half of Mary Catherine's 140 passengers. The average ages in second cabin and steerage were 22 and 24 and ½ years, indicating that the vast majority of immigrants left England in their prime, ready to begin new and productive lives in the New World.

Master Carr's entries show that thirty-five children (ages 16 and younger) traveled on the Mary Catherine with their families, mostly in steerage. One female passenger gave birth during the voyage, and fortunately, the infant arrived safely with its mother. One wonders how children fared on the long and potentially perilous trip to America. Although the first few days at sea may have been exhilarating for both adults and children, boredom undoubtedly set in quickly. Were the children free to roam, exploring the decks above and below? Did the parents entertain their toddlers with stories, games, or songs? But, as my wife once said, entertaining children was not a parental expectation in the 1800s. It seems far more likely that the children on the Mary Catherine were expected to lie quietly in their bunks and avoid the adults.

Much like the cruise ships that spread COVID-19 during the 2020-2023 pandemic, ships like the Mary Catherine could serve as fertile incubators for measles, smallpox, pneumonia, and other infectious diseases, especially for the children and adults traveling in steerage. Fortunately, no child died during the Mary Catherine's voyage to America. Such was not the case with numerous other transatlantic crossings. Grieving parents would be forced to place their dead children in crude wood coffins and watch grimly as the ship's carpenter drilled holes in the coffins and added sand to ensure that the small bodies sank to the ocean floor. How sad the funerals at sea must have been!

The majority of Mary Catherine's passengers hailed from England, but a few traveled from Scotland, Wales, Ireland, or the Isle of Man, an island nation located in the Irish Sea between Northern Ireland and England. Although most listed the U.S. as their final destination, some would head to Canada, and a few were bound for points unknown. In total, the Mary Catherine's passengers brought many essential skills to America, including carpentry, masonry, tailoring, accounting, and the law. More than a few men came with their wives and children. All arrived with the expectation of finding new, fulfilling lives in the New World.

After three years in New York, the Taylors ventured west to the Michigan Territory in 1835, two years before Michigan joined the Union. Michigan had been slated for statehood in 1835, but its entry into the Union had been delayed by the "Toledo War," a bloodless dispute that arose over a disagreement about the boundary between the Territory of Michigan and the State of Ohio. Michigan's politicians coveted the port of Toledo, and the youthful territorial governor, Stevens T. Mason, lobbied for a southern boundary that would provide the people of Michigan with convenient access to Lake Erie and the Maumee River, the largest river entering the Great Lakes. By contrast, Ohio, which had been granted statehood in 1803, would not relinquish Toledo.

When the U.S. Congress finally negotiated a treaty, Toledo and the Maumee River remained in Ohio. In return, Michigan received a wilderness tract of land that would become the western two-thirds of the state's Upper Peninsula, or U.P., for short. Although Mason and his fellow Michiganders felt cheated by the exchange, the state would ultimately benefit immensely from the U.P.'s rich iron and copper deposits.

James arrived first, settling in Spring Arbor, a tiny hamlet west of Jackson, Michigan, known for its numerous artesian springs. After finding sufficient work there as a tailor and confirming that the region was safe and hospitable, James retraced his journey to New York and returned to Michigan with his wife and young daughter. In 1837, the year of Michigan's statehood, the Taylor family moved to Concord, a village five miles west of Spring Arbor, where they built their home. There, James opened a tailor shop and owned the area's first sewing machine. Both his surname and upbringing in Macclesfield made tailoring the logical occupation for James.

The modest house that James and Rachel built, which would be inherited later by a Taylor daughter who married into the Reynolds family, sat on a knoll overlooking the Concord millpond of the Kalamazoo River. According to the historian Linda Hass, the Taylor's house on the hill became known for "offering hospitality, joy, and comfort." And as opposition to slavery grew, especially among Michigan's white citizens, the house became a refuge for runaway black slaves traveling north on the Underground Railroad.

Kalamazoo River, near Concord, Michigan
Source: The author

9

The Underground Railroad

My boyhood home in Three Oaks, Michigan
Source: The author

Growing up in southwest Michigan in the 1950s and early 1960s, I had no black friends and only a limited understanding of segregation and slavery in the U.S. Most of my friends traced their ancestors to England, Ireland, or Scandinavia, and at that, only a few had surnames suggesting German, Italian, or Polish heritage.

When we played baseball on the diamond behind the red brick high school in Three Oaks, we pretended to be Mickey Mantle, Roger Maris, Al Kaline, or another of our white idols, rather than Jackie Robinson, Willie Mays, Hank Aaron, or any of the talented black players who had finally broken Major League Baseball's color barrier. My best friend in sixth grade became Whitey Ford, and as I crouched behind home plate ready to receive his fastball, my short, squat build aptly earned me the nickname Yogi. I recall no bias in our actions; we simply had no experiences that enabled us to behave differently.

When I first learned about the Underground Railroad in elementary school, it almost seemed like a fairy tale. I could not comprehend how tunnels could be dug in the U.S. from south to north. Because I had traveled with my parents through Detroit's Windsor Tunnel, I wanted to believe that such a massive undertaking was possible. But I still could not imagine people traveling in countless tunnels beneath the Ohio River and through the hill country of eastern Kentucky.

Like most of my classmates, I had taken the words literally, not yet appreciating that the Underground Railroad was a wonderful metaphor for the perilous journey that brought runaway slaves north to freedom. And not until 2005, when my mother first showed me the photo of the Taylor-Reynolds house, did I begin to learn about slavery, the Underground Railroad, and the good deeds of my ancestors.

From the earliest days of their coerced, unpaid labor, slaves yearned to escape from bondage. The words "let my people go" seemed to apply equally well to the American slaves as they did to the Israelites who suffered under the Pharaoh's rule. Until the courageous acts of Harriet Tubman, who led numerous slaves north to freedom between 1849 and 1855, and Abraham Lincoln, who signed the emancipation proclamation in 1863, American slaves had no Moses to further their cause. How many American slaves successfully escaped their masters or died in the search for freedom prior to the establishment of the Underground Railroad remains open to question. Equally uncertain is the number of slaves who chose death by suicide as the means to end their suffering.

By the year 1700, more than half of the original thirteen colonies (Maryland, Massachusetts, Connecticut, New Jersey, New York, Pennsylvania, and Virginia) had legalized slavery, and several had statutes that benefited slave owners by imposing bounties for the capture and return of runaway slaves. New York, fearing the loss of its slave-heavy workforce, enacted legislation in 1705 that prohibited slaves from traveling to Canada, where they could find freedom. At the time, slaves constituted an essential labor pool in the colony, with more than 40% of the households in New York City possessing slaves as laborers or domestic servants, a prevalence rivaling that of Charleston, South Carolina, the epicenter of slavery in the South.

When the U.S. Constitution was ratified in 1788, Article IV, Section 2, Clause 3, gave slave owners the right to retrieve their property.

> No Person held to Service or Labour in one State, under the Laws thereof, escaping into another, shall, in Consequence of any Law or Regulation therein, be discharged from such Service or Labour, but shall be delivered up on Claim of the Party to whom such Service or Labour may be due.

Although the Constitution provided for the return of slaves to their owners, the emerging abolitionist movement in the north prompted U.S. congressmen from the south, who viewed slavery as vital to the region's economy, to lobby for passage of the Fugitive Slave Act of 1793. This act supplemented the Constitution by specifying the process by which slave owners could identify and retrieve runaway slaves. Moreover, the act imposed civil penalties, $500 for each offense (equal to $15,000 in 2023), on persons who concealed slaves and helped them escape.

The second and final Fugitive Slave Act, enacted by the U.S. Congress in 1850, sought to appease southern slave owners and dissuade slave states from seceding from the Union. The act increased the penalty for assisting runaway slaves to $1000, imposed a six-month prison sentence on persons convicted of harboring fugitive slaves, and limited the rights of runaway slaves by denying them access to jury trials. Federal agents enforced the 1850 law and received payment for each slave they returned to its owner. Rather than reducing the tension between free and slave states, the act amplified the cultural divide between the North and the South and prompted some free states, such as Wisconsin and Vermont, to pass statutes that counteracted federal law. And, as history tells us, the southern states would nonetheless secede from the Union.

With congressional empowerment, slave hunting in the mid-1800s became a lucrative cottage industry in which unscrupulous individuals, mostly white men, captured and returned runaway slaves to their masters. In their most egregious actions, slave hunters occasionally kidnapped free black men living in free states and forced them into slavery. Once 'home', the returned slaves faced cruel punishment designed to discourage other slaves from considering an escape. In some instances, public whipping or lynching led to the death of a returned slave, a tragic end to the slave's courageous action.

As tensions over slavery escalated in the 1850s, northern abolitionists became increasingly vocal in their opposition to slavery, and despite the penalties for aiding runaway slaves, many Michiganders, like my ancestors, became active participants in the Underground Railroad. As the Underground Railroad expanded, northbound routes appeared in several states, including Ohio, Indiana, New York, and Michigan. All routes led to Canada, the final destination, where black slaves would find freedom. Canada, a British colony at the time, did not honor the provisions of the Fugitive Slave Act and did not extradite runaway slaves to the U.S.

"Conductors," such as Harriet Tubman, led the slaves north to freedom, finding safe houses ("stations") maintained by abolitionist sympathizers ("station masters"), like the Taylors. In some places along their journey, slaves on the Underground Railroad might mingle in plain sight with fellow passengers, both black and white, as they traveled from station to station on the Freedom Trail. But in most instances, slaves traveled secretly by night and hid in a station's attic or cellar, fearful that slave hunters would discover and capture them before they could reach Canada.

From the work of Linda Hass, the historian of Jackson, Michigan, I learned that the Taylors had three locations in which they could hide runaway slaves. These included: a small cellar, which was accessed from the main floor of the farmhouse by a secret trap door; a dark closet, hidden beneath the stairway, which led to the farmhouse's second floor; and another tiny closet, just large enough for one person, above the rustic addition on the west end of the main house.

Although I know where the Taylors hid the runaway slaves, I know far less about the reasons they joined the Underground Railroad. What were their motives, and why did they risk fines or imprisonment? The $1000 fine specified by the Fugitive Act of 1850 seems unimaginably punitive given the wages that a tailor might receive. At the time, a textile worker in America received just $50 for a month's work. Yet, the Taylors still provided refuge.

I believe that the Taylor's upbringing in Macclesfield, England, laid the foundation for their actions. As in many English communities, organized religion, both Catholic and Protestant, greatly influenced the beliefs and behaviors of Macclesfield's residents, including the families of James and Rachel. Moreover, English churches in numerous towns sponsored "Sunday schools," which provided a sound moral education to the community's children on Sundays, the only day off for the youth who toiled in the factories.

In 1812, Macclesfield's Sunday School committee, an ecumenical organization, established the Big Sunday School. Its goal was to educate the town's children in reading, writing, and ciphering (i.e., mathematics), as well as to provide them with grounding in Christian principles. Here, James and Rachel likely learned how to read and write. They also benefited from numerous other important lessons, including the meaning of the "Golden Rule," the practice of treating others as you would want to be treated.

James and Rachel Taylor's decision to reside in rural southeast Michigan reinforced, I believe, their desire to help others. Living first in Spring Arbor, a tiny hamlet near the site of a Native American village, and then settling in Concord, the Taylors found like-minded people who valued human life and individual freedoms. By virtue of their location at the edge of the wilderness, Spring Arbor and Concord attracted numerous missionaries who brought the Word of God to the settlers drawn to the area by Michigan's impending statehood. Central to the religious teachings was the belief that all men (and women, too) were equal in the eyes of the Lord, regardless of the color of their skin. These kind and virtuous people became the Taylor's friends and neighbors.

Two of the area's early settlers, Benjamin Packard and William

Smith, platted the village of Spring Arbor in 1835 and planned for a Methodist school, which would provide a Christian education to the inhabitants of the rapidly-growing region. While neither the seminary nor the village of Spring Arbor materialized, Packard and Smith's vision for higher education served as the impetus for the founding of Albion College, the institution that would be located in Albion, Michigan, my mother's birthplace, ten miles northwest of Spring Arbor.

Among the many religious groups attracted to the area were the Free Will Baptists, a sect linked to the larger Baptist community by a belief in religious liberty. Two factions of the Free Will Baptist Church emerged in America, one in North Carolina and the other in New England. When their converts settled along the Kalamazoo River, they spread the gospel westward into Michigan. Like Packard and Smith, the Baptist ministers hoped to construct a seminary to promulgate their religious beliefs. To achieve these goals, the Free Will Baptists opened Central Michigan College in Spring Arbor in 1844, and in the manner of Packard and Smith, they subsequently relocated their institution to a larger village, Hillsdale, Michigan, 20 miles south. There, the school became known as Hillsdale College.

Not only did the missionaries mold the religious beliefs of the Taylors and other families living in the area, they also began to influence the social norms and politics of the region. With its roots in Spring Arbor's Free Will Baptist faith, Hillsdale College became the first U.S. college to prohibit discrimination on the basis of sex, religion, or race, and in the process, Hillsdale became just the second U.S. college to offer a four-year degree to women. Not to be outdone, Albion College became co-educational in the 1850s, and in 1861, Michigan's legislature approved the college's request to grant four-year liberal arts degrees to both men and women.

As early as the mid-1830s, the Free Will Baptists opposed slavery, calling it evil, but they did so cautiously, believing that the immediate and complete abolition of slavery posed far greater social problems than its gradual elimination. Many others, including Abraham Lincoln, shared this opinion, at least early on. Before long, however, the Free

Will Baptists pivoted and began to call for the immediate emancipation of all slaves, basing their revised stance on the words of the Bible. They joined with other American religious groups, most notably the Quakers, to become vocal participants in the abolitionist movement.

In the ensuing years, antislavery sentiments spread widely, becoming the prevailing opinion among people in the northern states, especially those living in southeast Michigan. In the mid-1850s, the state's abolitionists met in Jackson, Michigan, 15 miles east of Concord, to protest the passage of the Nebraska-Kansas Act, federal legislation that violated the antislavery provisions of the Missouri Compromise. In doing so, the protestors established the forerunner of the Republican Party, and Abraham Lincoln soon became its spokesperson as well as the Republican candidate for president. I do not know if the Taylors participated in the Jackson rally, but I have little doubt that they agreed with its objectives.

In Spring Arbor and Concord, the Taylors heard a chorus of moral voices that led them to the most compelling action. They had an obligation, I believe, to join the Underground Railroad and assist runaway slaves in their quest for freedom. The religious traditions of the Taylor's upbringing in England and the beliefs of their neighbors in Spring Arbor and Concord would not allow them to do otherwise. The Taylors had learned that freedom belonged to everyone, regardless of sex, religion, or race.

I now understand that the Underground Railroad was not a myth but a courageous act of civil disobedience. Justice and freedom were its objectives. Aided by the Taylors and countless other abolitionists, the Underground Railroad ultimately transported more than 100,000 southern slaves north to freedom. The Taylor's decision to join the Underground Railroad was the morally correct one, despite the dangers it posed, and I am extremely proud of their participation.

In the summer of 2019, six months before the COVID-19 pandemic temporarily took control of our lives, my wife and I drove Concord's tree-lined streets in search of the Taylor-Reynolds home. Knowing that the house overlooked the town's millpond, we thought that we had found it in a small clapboard house that stood on a knoll south of the pond. Later that day, we stopped at a bridge over the Kalamazoo River and paused to envision how runaway slaves might have traveled upriver to the house in their quest for freedom.

We would subsequently learn from my cousin Kim that the house had actually sat on the north side of the pond. Sadly, a new owner, who did not appreciate the historical significance of the property, demolished the house several years ago. All that remains now are an empty lot, a faded photograph, and my admiration for the Taylor's courage and resourcefulness. And the knowledge that my mom told the truth . . . this time.

Concord, Michigan, downtown, present day
Source: The author

10

⚜

The Truth

Michigan State Police of the Paw Paw post investigated the fatal shooting of James Bale Sr. at his farm on US12 east of Paw Paw to determine whether the 48 year old farmer committed suicide or met his death through an accident.

Bale's body was discovered Friday noon in a corn crib at the rear of the barn by his son James Jr. 20. Part of his head had been shot off and a 12 gauge shotgun lay by his side. Although he had been ill for sometime members of his family told State Police that they did not believe his illness caused him to commit suicide, and knew of no other reasons why he might have shot himself. Bale is survived by a wife, son and a daughter, all of whom reside on the farm east of Paw Paw.

South Haven Daily Tribune. Tuesday, September 23, 1943

Mom may have realized that I would eventually learn the truth about my grandfather's death, but I was 22 years old before she finally told me. I had just been accepted to the University of Michigan Medical School, and because my acceptance brought the privilege of 'being in medicine', she concluded that it was finally time. She told me that his death had most likely been a suicide, but because my dad had never discussed his father's death and she had never asked, she lacked additional details. She deflected my probing questions, saying only how sorry she felt for her husband, who had found his father, the man he loved most dearly, dead in a corn crib. We never again discussed his death.

My grandfather, James Sheldon Bale, the only son of Waldwin James and Clara Belle Sheldon Bale, was born on the Bale farm in 1894. He grew up at The Maples, learning how to farm, hunt, and navigate the world from Wally, his father, and Grandpa Bale, his grandfather, who still lived at the farm. My grandfather initially attended Richmond School, a one-room school house in Antwerp Township, and he eventually graduated from Paw Paw High School in 1914 at the age of 20. I found no obvious explanation why he seemed older than the typical Paw Paw High School graduate. The letters he wrote to my future grandmother, Blanche, suggest that he tolerated school primarily to participate in sports.

A handsome young man with an athlete's swagger, James Sheldon stood 6' 2" and towered over the comely Blanche, who was 5' 4", and her sister, Claribel, who was barely 5 feet tall. He pitched for the high school baseball team and also ran track. As a young man, he was the 'county miler', representing Van Buren County in races against runners from other Michigan communities. He once ran a mile in 4 minutes and 30 seconds, which seems remarkable given that the world record at the time, held by Norman Taber of the United States, was 4 minutes and 12.6 seconds.

More than 20 years elapsed between his days as an elite athlete and September 19, 1943, the day of his death. In the intervening years, he worked the farm, survived the Great Depression, weathered the drought and heat of the dust bowl days, and with Blanche, his beloved wife, raised two children, a daughter, Carol, their firstborn, and a son, my father, whom they named James Jr. Thus, my father became the fourth generation of Bales to bear the given name of James. In 1949, I became the fifth.

James Sheldon Bale, my grandfather, in track
attire, date unknown
Source: Unknown photographer

To the best of my knowledge, my grandfather did not leave a suicide note. It seems possible, however, that a note could have been left and discovered by Claribel, his adoring sister-in-law, who was the second person to arrive at the gruesome scene. After hearing the shotgun blast, his son, later to be my dad, found him first, and in his horror, he called Aunt Claribel to the corn crib. Because she is gone, too, we will never know if she found a note and destroyed it. In reality, though, people who die by suicide infrequently leave notes explaining their actions.

Grandma Bale fortunately saved twenty-four letters that my grandfather had written to her during their courtship. I do not know if she did so selectively, choosing only those that had the greatest meaning and helped her understand his suicide, or if she preserved them all. Did she cherish and reread them often after his death, or were they locked away until her own death in 1986, more than forty years after her husband's passing?

When I inherited the Bale family's Victorian walnut secretary after my own father's death, I discovered the letters in the secretary's lower section. I never learned who had placed them there or if anyone other than my grandmother had read them. My retirement in 2018 brought the opportunity to study the letters, and with the isolation necessitated by the COVID-19 pandemic, I began to write in 2020, hoping to reconstruct the story of why my grandfather took his own life.

The letters began in 1912, when James was 18 years old and a high school junior. Blanche, now 20 years old, has graduated from high school and anticipates enrolling in Western States Normal School in the fall of that year. James wrote some letters during class time, and others he wrote in his room late at night after he had completed his exhausting farm chores. He composed the first letter in the collection late on July 29, 1912, a Sunday night. He had just returned to The Maples during a thunderstorm and wrote . . . "The lightning did crash, the thunder roll, and the rain fell in torrents" . . . and he then described a near calamity with Duke, his horse.

> I had reached home and was unhitching Duke. I had one side all loose when the handle of the lantern I had in my hand touched him on his side and he started to leave in a hurry but I managed to get hold of his bridle in time to stop his tipping the buggy over for it was about ready to go.

It was nine PM when he finished his letter, closing with:

the old clock has just struck nine so I must quit my scribbling and go to bed like a good little boy or five o'clock will come too quick which it most always does. As ever, Jimmy.

In the next letter, dated October 1, 1912, we learn that school has resumed (*James is a high school junior*), and the first few weeks had not gone well for James.

How do you like your school now? (*Blanche is now in college studying toward a teacher's certificate.*) I think I will have to quit for I expect to get about three warnings this month. I have always heard that the freshman year was always the hardest but not as much with me as this year is the hardest . . . or is starting out bad enough now.

We also learn that Blanche frequently wrote to James, but sadly, we have none of her letters.

P.S. I got your letter last week as Claribel said you were afraid that the other James Bale might open as it did not have Jr. or Sr. So I thought that I would let you think he did until now . . . for she (*Claribel*) said that you were very much alarmed about it . . . JB

Just as it was for me and my dad in Three Oaks and later, in Rockford, being Junior and Senior James Bales at The Maples had its complications. (*For that matter, the many Bale generations with a son named James have confused just about everyone.*) James wrote the next letter two weeks later.

Mattawan, Michigan, Oct. 15, 1912. I will at least try and answer your letter but I can hardly write as I hurt my first two fingers on my right hand so it is hard to hold the pen. Those Sophs put it over on us Juniors again to-night (I will not tell the score as it was very one sided). Mr. Meyer umpired and he is certainly a college bum out of school if there ever was one . . . I tried to drop geometry again and Mr. Robertson asked me what I was going to be and I said "Sodbuster" . . .

Last Saturday I thought my days were numbered all right for a few minutes anyway. I had drawn grapes from the vineyard all day with Dandy (*another of the Bale's horses*) and when the bell rang (*ending the day's picking*) I had another load to get and this made him mad and he did not want to go when I was going out to the vineyard . . . so I hit him with the end of the lines and you can imagine my surprise when he kicked up and if the load had not held him down, I would have had his feet in my face . . . Yours, J. S. B. Jr.

So, peril existed not only for the Junior and Senior Bales, but also between a man and his horse.

Mattawan, Mich. Nov. 5, 1912. I don't know whether or not it is my time to write but anyhow I will write a few lines. I reached home safely Sunday night after a nice walk from Mattawan . . . (*about four miles*) . . . The Juniors defeated the Freshman tonight by a score of 11 or 12 to 1. They beat us before and they said that they hoped that I would pitch this game as I was easy, but I got mad enough so that I could pitch. It looked in the first inning as if they would beat us again for I gave the first man up a base on balls. Then Claude (*the catcher*) dropped the third strike on the next man so he got to first, then I hit the next man up so the bases were full with no men out. The next thing I did was to get mad and strike out the next three men and they did not score . . . will write soon, J. S. B. Jr.

Here, we learn that he had a temper, although it seemed that he could focus his emotions. Did his temper erupt at other times? Perhaps when channeling the energy was more difficult?

Mattawan, Michigan, Nov. 17, 1912. This is Sunday night and I have been very very good and went to church . . . I am sick because us Juniors let those Seniors beat us last Friday night by a score of 2 to 0. It should have been our game . . . the night before Thanksgiving J --- G---- is going to have a box social and he wants all of the Paw Paw bunch that will and can to go . . . will you go to that social . . . with me? . . . I have a confession to make to you. Last Sunday night I was with a girl and it was no one else than your little sister Claribel. I asked her if she wanted to go riding and she said that she would so we went out west of town . . . the next Monday L---- made more sport than a little at me for being with C. J. B. Jr.

Mattawan, Mich. Nov. 20, 1912. Dear Blanche. I received your letter today and am answering it now. We are all going out to Kalamazoo . . . and I will come up to see if I can find where you live. I would have written you before but I supposed you were coming home as I would not need it. If I write any more I will freeze as it is cold up here in my room. Yours J. B. Jr.

The next letter, written sometime after the Thanksgiving get-together, provides the first hint of tension in their relationship. Sadly, I lack Blanche's letter to know what she had written. To this day, I do not know if James or anyone else saved any of her letters.

> Mattawan, Mich. Feb. 15, 1913. Dear Blanche. I will try to answer your letter that came yesterday. I know not hardly what to say, but what I do say, take it as the truth . . . I thought that Claribel might like a ride . . . and she said she would so we went riding and then went to church. We only went out west of town 2 miles. Now please do not think that it was Claribel's fault for it was not . . . it was mine, so don't be angry with her . . . I was to blame. I always have been a fool and guess always will be.
>
> You said in your letter that "perhaps it would be better if we did not go together anymore" but before you make up your mind for sure please read "The Rosary" (a poem) . . . very carefully and after that if your conscience tells you that you are right about being angry with me for last Sun. and I am wrong.

James' wrote this letter in large cursive letters that were noticeably different than his handwriting in all of the other letters. Even without reading the words, I could see his emotions on every page. Midway through the letter, he abruptly changed the subject, and this, too, seems to provide insight. Was the thought of losing Blanche simply too painful for him to continue?

> You spoke about my "making a record next spring" in your letter but the only record I will ever make is that at getting hurt. Papa went to church one night last week and I had to do his chores and one cow kicked only six times in about the same place every time on my left

leg . . . then a week ago tonight Duke (*the horse*) kicked me on my right leg and if had hit me only four inches lower it would probably have broken my leg . . . yours, Jas. S. Bale

After an unexplained gap, James wrote again, this time from school.

Mattawan, Michigan. May 26, 1913. I will now try to answer your letter that I received some time ago. I would have answered it before but have been very busy so have not had time. This is the last hour in the afternoon at 2:30 that I am writing this and the girl that sits in front of me is around so that she keeps my desk in motion as the screws that hold it the floor are loose and some are gone so you will have to excuse such bad writing . . . You asked me in that letter what we were doing in athletics . . . well, we had an inter-class meet one week ago today and we Juniors won by about 67 to 29 . . . how is school at the Norm now? (*Blanche was attending Western State Normal School in Kalamazoo working toward a teaching certificate.*) . . . same as ever I suppose.

The subsequent letters in the collection begin in early 1916. James has finished high school and now farms at The Maples, while Blanche lives in Port Huron, Michigan. She has completed her education, anticipates receiving a temporary teaching certificate, and has accepted summer employment in Port Huron, a city of 20,000 located at the southern-most tip of Lake Huron, more than 200 miles from Paw Paw. Port Huron lies about as far east as one could travel in Michigan without crossing into Canada. Was this the only work that Blanche could find, or does her location speak volumes about their relationship?

The next letter, written just before Blanche left for Port Huron, provides the most vivid description of James' emotions and his thoughts about their relationship.

> Mattawan Mich. June 14, 1916. Dear Blanche: Since I am not going to see you tonight I will have to write you a letter even if you do not get it until tomorrow . . . how are you? Working hard as usual I suppose. I worked until 10 o'clock last night getting seed potatoes ready to plant today, also our alfalfa is out in this rain. I cut it Tuesday morning as I did not expect it to rain . . .

> Blanche, do you know it makes me feel lonesome when I think of your going away this summer . . . what will I do when you are gone for two months or more? I do not know why, but I almost feel it that if you do go away that something will happen between us and that would be terrible (for me any how). I almost think sometimes it would be better for you if I did disappear but I would just not do it now because Blanche I do love you so much, more than I can tell about.

And what did my grandfather mean when he wrote that it might be better for him to disappear? From her life? Or did his words suggest something else? He continued:

> So Blanche please think hard before you go away of me and of all that you may come in contact while there for you know that a city is a bad bad place for a lone girl sometimes and think what would become of me if something should happen to you. Do not think that it is just my selfishness that I don't want you to go but look ahead and think of the people that you will meet, people who would not hesitate in the least to hurt a girls

life when you are so pure and nice . . . yours, Jimmie B. P.S. you had better destroy this for someone else might find it. J

But Blanche did not destroy the letter of June 14, 1916. Because of her inaction, I understand more clearly the intensity and perhaps the irrationality of my grandfather's emotions. This letter, more than any letter thus far, may provide insight into why he died by suicide. His letter suggests a growing dependence on Blanche. Two days later, he sent Blanche another letter.

> Mattawan, Mich. Sunday, June 16, 1916. My Dearest Blanche: Since I cannot talk to you I am doing the next best thing writing a letter. I was going to write yester-day but did not find time, or rather did not have a way of mailing a letter. How is the weather in Port Huron? It is awful hot here, we had a very very small shower this AM not enough to lay the dust long. It must be our neighborhood is very wicked for there has been rain all around us but not here and is very dry.

James then asked Blanche if she received her licenses, although he didn't elaborate on their purpose. (*I suspect that she was awaiting her college certificate and state license to teach school.*) He wrote that if they don't come, she'd better come home.

> You may be sure that I would be very very very very very very very very very glad to see you for you have been gone for a long time now.

This letter, which ran twelve pages, also mentioned the suicide of a mutual acquaintance, a young woman who apparently lived in the Paw Paw area.

> It is very sad about Miss B------. You may be sure that I would feel very very sad if you should do such a thing but you may be sure that I will never give you cause for such a thing like D---- did. I think it will be lesson for him don't you? Not to treat love so lightly especially after he is engaged to a girl.

Later in the same letter, he reflected again on the impact of the young woman's suicide on D----, and this time, he provided some insight into his own feelings.

> Also it is very unlucky that Miss B------ killed herself, for D---- I think, for he will be known by people who never heard of him before as the man who caused her death . . . it will be hard for him to get away from it, hard to forget it, at least it would be for me, in fact I don't think I ever could.

I can only guess how Blanche reacted when she read James' letter. Did she cry out, as I did, "But what about the young woman and her family?" What did the letter tell her about the man she would eventually marry? The next letter was written slightly more than a week later.

> Mattawan, Mich. June 25, 1916. "Dear Blanche: . . . Blanche, do you know that this is the first Sunday we have not seen each other since last August . . . I have thought of you all this time wondering how you have been spending the days. Mr. E--- came over today . . . We went over to the place and he told me that I am a joke as a farmer and that he wants nothing more to do with me

. . . I mean that is what I expected he would tell me but it was just the opposite he though that the crops were look fairly good and I was doing the best that could be done under the circumstances . . . and we will paint the house and barn and fix things up a little . . . he told me that I would have to "get married and live on the place" and I said that that was what I am expecting to do.

Although James' comment about being a "joke" as a farmer may have been written in jest, this and other statements suggest that he had little confidence in his ability as a farmer. I suspect that he pined for the success of his father, Wally, and his talented grandfather, Grandpa Bale, but I doubt that he ever found it. James' insecurity seemed to extend well beyond his relationship with Blanche.

Mattawan, Mich. Monday Afternoon, June 26, 1916. Dear Blanche: It rains, so we are having a little vacation. I thought that we were at last going to get that last field of alfalfa drawn into the barn but there is a load and a half out yet and it rains like everything, now 3:45 PM. I received your letter today. I was very glad to hear from you (just as if you thought that I might not be) . . . Well I must stop or I will sleep until noon tomorrow and that would not do at all . . . write soon please. Your, very own, Jim B

Mattawan, Mich. July 2, 1916. My dear little girl: Since I cannot see you today, I am going to do the next best thing and that is write you a letter and I hope that you are also writing a letter and that I will be reading it about a day after tomorrow . . .

James then wrote about a detective story, "Who's Guilty?" from the local newspaper, that described a young woman who possessed a superb singing voice and wanted to tour the country. Her husband did not want her to go. In the end, she went to the city and met a composer who wanted her for his own. In the process of resisting his advances, she stabbed him, and he died. The husband, who loved his wife dearly, confessed to the crime rather than see her arrested and imprisoned.

> When I read this story, it made me think more than ever of the differences between you and I. You're so pure and fine and could rise much higher than I can ever hope to, for I am just one of the "below the ordinary fellows" while you are much above the ordinary. But Blanche, I cannot give up because I love you so much more than I ever dreamed that I could love a girl . . . hoping to get a fine long letter from you soon. I am your own. James.

Blanche was smart, too, graduating second in her high school class in 1912. Had she been a boy, I suspect that she would have been first. Not only do his letters reveal James' insecurity as a farmer, they also suggest that he had low self-esteem. Did these thoughts emerge later as depression, the reason for his suicide?

One comment, almost made as an afterthought in the July 2 letter, suggests that my father's vocal talents were inherited. James wrote:

> Mrs. C----- tried to get me to sing for them today but the horses were working Thursday and they were tired that night so I had a good excuse to go.

So, not only was my grandfather a superb athlete and hard worker, he could sing, too! James' next letter was written three days later.

Mattawan, Mich. July 5. 1916. Dear Blanche: Although it is 9:15 I am going to write a short letter to you . . . Blanche you want to appreciate this letter greatly for I have been somewhat busy today for I got up at 4:30, was out cultivating potatoes at 6:00 until 7:30 then went over to Alice's and raked hay until noon then drew hay this afternoon and I got home at 7:45, then ate my supper, and hitched up Molly (*another of the Bale's horses*) again and raked hay until dark and then did my chores and it was 9:00. Do you see I have been busy but I am not tired . . . you asked about my losing sleep going to see you, when you were home, dear I do not begrudge the sleep that I lose because I go to see you or write you a letter . . . your own, Jimmie

Blanche remained in Port Huron, although we never learned her reason for not returning promptly to Paw Paw. James soon wrote another 10 page letter.

Mattawan, Mich. July 9, 1916. Dear Blanche: . . . you asked how many nights I worked after supper last week. I don't know myself, so can't tell you. You say I work too hard? You don't know me as well as you think. I have not done half as much as I should so I guess I have not done too much . . . You asked why I think that there is such a difference between us. If you could have seen me yesterday you would have known. I was pitching hay and it was awful hot. If you have ever seen anyone who has fallen into the water and then rolled in some clover chaff you can imagine how my clothes looked . . . in the barn it was very hot, and also I have not shaved since last Sunday, so I did not look very smooth . . . So honestly Blanche wouldn't you rather have a man who would wear white flannels in the summer time and look cool than a man who shows up at the house at noon and right from the field covered with dirt and dust? . . . I am quite sure that anyone that I have worked for can't say that I have quit a job just because it was hard.

And he continued:

It seems though that we were meant for each other for if we were not I am quite sure that we would never started going together again after quitting so long, don't you think so dear? I do.

So, this explains the nearly three-year gap in the letters. Blanche and James had apparently ended their relationship in 1913, only to begin seeing each other again in 1916.

Mattawan, Mich. July 12, 1916. Dear B.E.B.: At last we are almost thru haying only about half of a load out hoping that if it did it might rain and cool things off a little for it is awful hot. Do you know that I have pitched 43 loads of hay so far this summer and I suspect that we will have alfalfa enough yet to bring it up to 50, so you see I have done a little something . . . I cultivated corn this morning until 10 o'clock and then drew in hay. I would have drawn that other half load but Papa was almost "all in" as it was hot. I also cultivated corn this afternoon so you see I had ought to feel like letter writing tonight as I have not worked hard today . . .

In nearly anyone else's view, especially Blanche's, he worked excep-tionally hard. Is this yet another example of my grandfather's self-deprecating personality? James then described a chance meeting with a young woman.

> But dear you may be sure that I did not ask if I might go up to see her Sunday night. There is only one girl that I care to see on Sunday nights and that is your own dear self.

The next paragraph, which is a continuation of his July 12th letter, provides additional insight into Blanche's concerns about James' need to work long hours. Does this letter suggest that the long, exhausting hours of farm work would eventually take a physical and emotional toll on my grandfather and contribute to his suicide?

> Blanche I am surprised at you and in fact almost ashamed of you that you would even think that if I don't stop working that I will break down. I am only 21 years old but if I was 61, I would not be surprised at your thinking it, but now I am in good fighting condition, even if I am a little thin now. I will gain it back next winter.

The next paragraph in this letter implies that James had a well-defined view of the roles of women and men. His words likely reflected the prevailing opinions of the day and the growing controversy about women's rights. In 1920, just four years hence, the 19th Amendment would grant women the right to vote. Most women were still expected, even after this, to quit their jobs when they married. His words suggest that he had given the topic considerable thought and might even tolerate her pursuit of a teaching career.

> Do you think that if will be necessary of you to teach more than three years more? I hope that it won't. I hope

that I am not such a failure as all that, of course it would be nice for you to have a life certificate (*the eventual outcome of her education at Western Normal*) so if anything should happen to me later that you would have it if you should have to teach again.

Blanche Bale, my grandmother, upon receipt
of her permanent teaching certificate, 1930
Source: Unknown photographer

As it turned out, my grandmother's teaching certificate benefited the family financially during James' lifetime and provided her with steady income upon his death. In all, she would teach for 41 years. James closed the letter of July 12th with:

Please don't forget to write as I get very very very lonesome to see you, even if I have lots to do I think of you very very very often wishing you were home now. But I suppose that I will have to stand it until you get home. Jim

James wrote two more letters that summer, one on August 9th and the other on August 30^(th), both before Blanche's return to Paw Paw. He eagerly anticipates her arrival, but otherwise, the general themes of his letters remain much the same: long hours working at the farm and self-deprecation.

> Mattawan, Mich. August 9, 1916. Just 24 more days more and you will be home if you come home on the 2^(nd) (*of September*) and 31 if you wait a week more, it seems as if I can hardly wait until then and you may be very sure that James S. Bale will be right on hand when you land in Lawton unless something very great happens to him before then . . . you know we can never tell what will happen to us from one day to the next . . .
>
> I dug potatoes yesterday and that I would have it easy picking apples today, but I am lazier tonight than last night. I picked 9 barrels today and I think that there will be 10 or 11 more of the Dutchess. Apples seem scarce this year but of course there will have to be something wrong with mine so I don't get top price, they range from $3 to $5 (*a barrel*) in Chicago now (*Mattawan and Paw Paw lie approximately 92 miles east of Chicago by rail*).

The Dutchess apple, now rarely seen in grocery stores, originated in Russia as a cultivar known as the Dutchess of Oldenburg. Like spy apples, a related variety, Dutchesses made excellent sauce and pies, and like the Concord grapes they grew, the apples provided an important source of income for the Bales. Later in the letter of the 9^(th), James again addressed Blanche's employment.

> You are not planning to go South or West on that canvassing business this winter are you? I read your letter saying that you might go. I do not know what I would ever do if you should be gone as long as that for it seems ages since I saw you last, now. Last winter I would have

gone away to work if it had not been for you. I did not want to miss seeing you Sunday and Wed. nights and I love you more now (if it is possible to) than I did then dear.

Last night when I led Billy (*the horse*) out to water, I climbed on his back and rode him around the yard and he had only the halter on, too. He is like me I guess for he has spells of being ugly, or rather he is not as bad as I am for I am ugly all the time and he is only by spells.

Was "ugly" James' euphemism for anger, or was it something else? Does my grandfather's revelation provide insight into my own father's tendency to lose his temper abruptly?

James' wrote the last letter of the summer on August 30, 1916. Blanche apparently decided to stay in Port Huron for an additional week.

Mattawan, Mich. Aug. 30, 1916. Just one week from to-day and you will be home "you say" and I can hardly wait but I suppose I will have too . . . Just think, after this week I won't have to write so many letters and you won't either, to me, anyhow. I do not mind writing twice a week but it will be seem much nicer to see you twice a week instead. . . . What time to you expect to arrive in Paw Paw? Or do you want me to meet you in Lawton as you spoke about before?

The next brief letter, written in pencil on both sides of a 3 x 5 inch note card, was sent from Lawton on January 17, 1917.

My dear little girl: Wednesday and it seems as if something is wrong because we are not together to-night.

James sent his subsequent letter in February. The pace of my grand-father's letter writing has apparently slowed due to Blanche's return to the Paw Paw area. This letter also comes from Lawton, where James was harvesting ice. There, he could also visit his sister Beatrice and her in-laws.

> Lawton, Mich. Thurs Feb. 1917. We finished drawing ice yesterday also we put the sawdust in and as a result I have a very lame back, or rather a very lazy back, it is not very lame. I should have enough ice for two loads up the chute out of the water into the wagon, alone. I didn't suspect I was strong enough but found out that I was. . .
>
> Mr. Thornton (*the father-in-law of his sister, Beatrice*) told me tonight that you have gone back on me because I have not had a letter from you this week, however, I still hope that there is a dear girl in Paw Paw that goes by the name of Blanche E. Buckley who be kind enough to let a little boy by the name of Jimmy Bale go to her home to see her next Sunday, if he manages to wait until then and if I cannot wait he will walk over some evening. . . Your very own. Jimmie Bale

In October and November 1917, James sent the final two letters in my grandmother's collection. Each letter contained tidbits of news and brief updates regarding my grandfather's work on the farm. In one letter, written on October 31, 1917, James expressed concern that the grapes, apples, pears, and almost himself were frozen, especially when a cow went missing.

> We did have a time finding that cow yesterday. We got lost in the swamp and I don't know what all.

Winter, a harsh season for Michigan farmers, had apparently arrived early that year.

Much to my surprise, James' final letters lacked any reference to his love for Blanche, his proposal of marriage, her acceptance, or their upcoming wedding. Pursuing Blanche, it seems, had been a race for him to win. And now he had crossed the finish line and would claim the prize.

My dad (center), his uncle Nat (left), my grandmother Blanche and my grandfather, James (far right) in 1937
Source: Unknown photographer

Less than a month later, Blanche and James were married in Paw Paw on November 25, 1917. James was 23 years old and Blanche had just turned 25 on November 23rd. Like many couples of the day, they honeymooned at Niagara Falls, New York. They also spent part of their time in central New York State where Blanche had lived with an aunt in Canastota, a village on the Erie Canal, during her middle and high school years. Bright, ambitious young women, like Blanche, sometimes went away for schooling in the early 1900s, I've been told, so that they could focus on their education. The couple would remain married and reside together at The Maples until James' death nearly 26 years later.

11

⧼❦⧽

Suicide

In 2021, the most recent year for which the Centers for Disease Control and Prevention have complete data, suicide claimed nearly 50,000 lives in the U.S., corresponding to approximately one death by suicide every 11 minutes. Non-Hispanic white men, like my grandfather, have the second highest suicide rate, 17.4 per 100,000, exceeded only by American Indian/Alaskan Native men, who have a rate more than 50% higher at 28.1 per 100,000. Men of all age groups outnumber women who die by suicide by a factor of nearly 4 to 1. Given the proliferation of guns in the United States, firearms are *by far* the most common method of suicide, accounting for more than 50% of cases, followed by suffocation (usually by hanging), 26%, and poisoning, 12%. During the past twenty years, the rate of suicide in the U.S. has risen by nearly 40%.

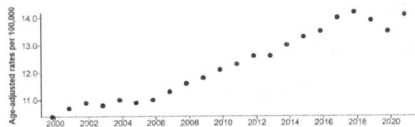

U.S. suicide rates during the past 20 years
Source: U. S. Centers for Disease Control and Prevention

The available information tells us that age, depression, alcoholism, and access to firearms all contribute to the risk of suicide. The sex of the individual is also a major factor. While far more men die by suicide, many more women attempt suicide. Teen suicides justifiably attract the greatest media attention, but suicide rates among U.S. residents are actually highest in people 85 years of age and older. Not far behind, however, are young and middle-aged people between the ages of 25 and 64. In neighboring Canada, men between the ages of 40 and 59 have the highest rate of suicide. My grandfather was in his late 40s when he took his own life.

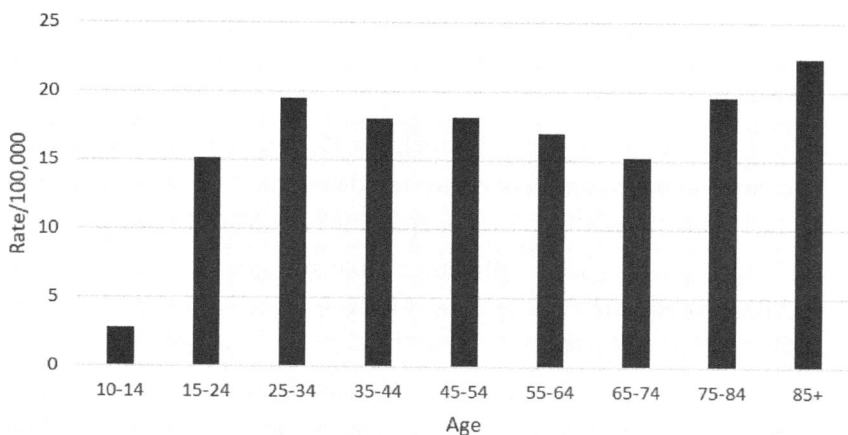

U.S. suicide rate by age (years)
Source: Data from the U.S. Centers for Disease Control and Prevention

When I joined the University of Iowa in the early 1980s as a junior faculty member in the Departments of Pediatrics and Neurology, a senior colleague occasionally came to my clinic to watch me work. In retrospect, I suspect that the chairman of pediatrics had assigned him the task of evaluating my clinical skills, but he never revealed this. Instead, he would engage me in stimulating discussions about my patients and frequently ask how I reached a particular diagnosis. I enjoyed our conversations immensely.

A year or so after our last interaction, he did not show up for work one morning. Later that day, they found his body in his garage with the car running; he had died from carbon monoxide poisoning. Next to him in the front seat of his car sat a bottle of his favorite whiskey and a short note stating that he believed that he had outlived his usefulness to others and decided to commit suicide. He lived alone, finding companionship only in the visits he made to the hospital and clinic. He was 80 years old.

When people leave suicide notes, they often describe how their possessions should be distributed and simply serve as holographic wills. Some notes indicate that behavioral health issues, especially depression, played a major role in the person's suicide. Even though my grandfather left no note, the letters that he wrote to my grandmother-to-be suggest that he was a fragile, self-deprecating man who had low self-esteem. Given this, he seemed prone to depression. His long hours as a laborer and the fatigue he experienced while working on the farm likely added to his distress, as my grandmother Blanche had astutely predicted early in their relationship.

The family's comments to the Michigan State Police indicate that my grandfather had not been feeling well for some time. Was he suffering from depression, or did he have an undiagnosed medical condition? Or was he simply exhausted, both physically and mentally? Was his striking forehead tan line, which I noted in every one of his adult photographs, just a farmer's tan, or could it have been a sign of hypothyroidism or adrenal insufficiency, uncommon medical disorders that can provoke depression? Because he did not undergo an autopsy, we will never know if a medical condition contributed to his suicide. I don't believe that alcohol was a factor, but then, I don't really know.

While farming, per se, does not impart as high a risk of suicide as some occupations, such as law enforcement or healthcare support, farmers frequently die by suicide, especially during difficult economic times. When we moved to Iowa City, Iowa, in 1982, the U.S. was in the midst of a farm crisis, and the mood among people in the farm community was sullen. And not infrequently, tragedies happened.

On the morning of December 9, 1985, Dale Burr, a 63-year-old man who farmed near Hills, Iowa, eight miles south of Iowa City, walked into the Hills Bank office with a 12-gauge shotgun, the same type of weapon that my grandfather used, and murdered John Hughes, the forty-six-year-old bank president. Earlier that morning, Burr had killed Emily, his wife of 40 years, while she was baking in the kitchen, and he then drove to Hills in his pickup truck and shot Hughes, a respected small-town banker who had worked diligently to help local farmers. Later that day, Burr murdered a neighboring farmer and then shot himself while sitting in the front seat of his truck near his home. He had just been stopped by a sheriff's deputy, who apparently sat nearby in his patrol car waiting for backup. At the time of his death, Burr owed more than $500,000 to various lenders, including Hills Bank.

In the 1980s, more than 1,000 farmers in the U.S. died by suicide because they anticipated losing their farms to foreclosure. Although the rate of suicide, as well as the number of farm foreclosures, has declined, many challenging issues still plague farmers, including fluctuating commodity prices, international trade disputes, and the weather. Farmers remain vulnerable to suicide because of the severe emotional impact of isolation, the physical pain associated with farming, and their limited access to behavioral health services. But they do have access to firearms, as did my grandfather, since shotguns and rifles are frequently kept on farms as tools, much like shovels, rakes, or hoes.

Farming, a demanding occupation, requires patience, perseverance, and resilience, behavioral characteristics that not all people possess. Moreover, farmers must be effective entrepreneurs. The Bale farm had prospered while his father and Grandpa Bale were alive, but my grandfather could not sustain their successes. Although his letters to Blanche confirm that he was a tireless worker, my grandfather seemed to lack the passion, or perhaps the ability, to manage the farm. He had also fallen victim to events he could not control, including the economic hardships of the Great Depression and the calamitous weather of the Dust Bowl days. My grandfather, it seems, was too proud to ask for help, not even from Blanche, his wife, despite the fact that she undoubtedly had many of the skills he needed. In his mind, he had failed, a conclusion that his competitive spirit could not handle. I truly believe that his perceived failure as a farmer led to a profound depression from which he never recovered.

At least my grandfather did not kill his son, later to be my father, or his sister-in-law, our beloved Aunt Claribel, who were both at the farm on that fateful day. As the tragic story of Dale Burr tells us, suicides on the farm can sometimes become murder-suicides.

In response to the needs of the farm community, many states and organizations, such as the State of Minnesota, where suicides among farmers reached epidemic proportions in the 1980s and 1990s, have created comprehensive programs to help farmers in distress. The Minnesota Department of Agriculture's elaborate website, *Coping with Farm and Rural Stress*, contains lifeline contacts (phone, text, and email) as well as links to financial advisors, educational materials, and behavioral health counselors who can provide confidential services at no cost. Had such support systems existed when my grandfather's life at The Maples began to spiral out of control, he may have lived to see all of his grandchildren.

Psychologists who study suicide give us several models to explain the complex behavioral factors that lead to suicide. The path to suicide often begins with feelings of inadequacy that prevent a person from meeting unrealistic life expectations. My grandfather's letters repeatedly revealed these characteristics. Loss of control or harm to one's self-image that evokes shame or humiliation accentuates the downward spiral. Finally, damage to relationships can be the pivotal event that precipitates suicide. While I have no information to suggest that my grandfather and grandmother experienced marital problems, the letters confirm that my grandfather James had 'lost' Blanche once during their courtship, and the thought of losing her again could have been overwhelming.

Another piece in the suicide puzzle is the effect that suicide in friends or acquaintances can have on a person's thought processes. In one of James' later letters, he discusses the death of Ms. B------. Although he focuses on the impact of her death on her fiancé, who apparently had committed an act of infidelity, James clearly inserted himself into the situation when he wrote:

> . . . for he will be known by people who never heard of him before as the man who caused her death . . . it will be hard for him to get away from it, hard to forget it, at least it would be for me, in fact I don't think I ever could.

Because the young woman's suicide occurred years before his own, James' suicide can't be considered a 'copycat' death, another important factor in suicidality. Nonetheless, my grandfather undoubtedly remembered the tragic event and knew that suicide can provide the opportunity to escape from severe psychological trauma or unbearable physical pain.

An issue that has troubled me for many years is the potential hereditary aspect of suicide. Numerous genetic studies suggest that suicidality, the thoughts and actions that lead to suicide, can be an inherited trait, with genetics contributing 17% to 55% of the risk that a person will attempt suicide. Let's put this another way. If heredity adds nothing to the risk of suicide, it's 0%. If, on the other hand, genetics accounts for all of the risk, it's 100%. So, while the available data don't tell the full story, they nonetheless suggest that heredity is an important factor.

To delve more deeply into the role of genetics in suicide, a multi-center research consortium investigated whether certain human genes might be associated with a suicide attempt. In 2022, they published the results of a genome-wide association study, better known by its abbreviation, GWAS, and reported that the risk of attempting suicide mapped to a position, known as a genetic locus, on chromosome 7. The linkage to chromosome 7 seemed independent of risk-taking behavior, major depression, smoking, or other factors that can be linked to a heightened suicide risk.

A subsequent study of suicide among military veterans, published in 2023, not only supports the linkage of suicidal thoughts and behaviors to chromosome 7, but also suggests that the regulation of certain genes on this chromosome, including SLC4A2, CDK5, PDE3A, and RAR-RES3, may have a role in suicidality. This study, known as a methylation study, investigated how the sites of gene regulation, which occurs by the biochemical process called methylation, might be associated with suicide.

Of these genes, CDK5, a cyclin-dependent kinase gene, sparked the greatest interest among the geneticists and psychiatrists who conducted the study. This gene, present in human brain tissue, appears to regulate several key brain and nerve cell (neuronal) functions, including neuronal growth and survival, learning and memory, and circadian rhythms. Impaired regulation of CDK5 has been detected in Alzheimer and Parkinson diseases, major degenerative disorders in humans. Moreover, GWAS studies have identified associations between CDK5 and other brain disorders, including schizophrenia, attention-deficit hyperactivity disorder, and depression.

While these results seem promising, much more work is needed to clarify the neurogenetics and neurobiology of suicide and the role played by specific genes. Thus far, scores of genes have been associated with suicide attempts or death by suicide, indicating that suicide represents a highly complex human disorder. And like many other complex human disorders, such as autism spectrum disorder, obesity, and hypertension, suicide displays genetic heterogeneity, the phenomenon in which multiple different genes contribute to the occurrence of a single condition. If future studies bear fruit, we can hope that analyzing our DNA may someday identify the people who have the greatest suicide risk.

While I am not aware of any other suicides in our family, my review of Ilfracombe's historical records disclosed occasional instances of suicide, even in the 1800s. I found one case especially disturbing, even though I know of no connection with our family other than the man's name. That said, is it possible that my distant grandfather, William Bale, or one of his daughters died by suicide?

WILLIAM BALE, of Glendower-cottage, the Tors, Lyn-mouth, committed suicide on Wednesday afternoon by cutting his throat with a razor. Deceased was about thirty-two years of age, married, and had one child. He was a painter by trade, and used to occupy his slack time by waiting at the Cottage and other hotels during the season. BALE'S little child told her mother that "daddy" would not speak to her, and MRS BALE on going upstairs was shocked to find her husband lying face downward with the razor by his side. Her husband had been considerably depressed lately, and she believed his depression was greatly the result of a bad attack of in-fluenza, which he had at Christmas. In the morning he offered a very fervent prayer in the kitchen, asking the Lord to give him strength. She asked him what troubled him, and he replied that "There was nothing."

One of the more complicated aspects of a very complex disorder is the impact that suicide has on the surviving friends and family members. Each affected individual has a uniquely personal relationship with the person who dies, and this relationship affects how the survivors process the event. As we learned years ago from the groundbreaking work of Elisabeth Kubler-Ross, grief, the overarching emotion felt by survivors, has several elements, among them denial, anger, depression, and acceptance. Survivors experience some or all of these emotions, and the intensity and duration of each emotion can vary considerably for each survivor. Many survivors also feel considerable guilt and may blame themselves for not taking action to prevent the suicide. Such emotions can persist for years and may even span generations.

I'm certain that the Bale family, especially my grandmother, aunt, father, and great aunt, suffered greatly after my grandfather's death. This alone may explain why my grandmother often seemed distant. Was she paralyzed by the fear of losing other people she loved? Was she seeing her husband every time she looked at her children and grandchildren? Did she harbor guilt for his action? Or was there something else?

I can't imagine how my father coped with the horrifying experience of hearing the shotgun blast and then finding his father's bloody body. I occasionally heard my dad crying softly, most often in the evening, as he sat alone in my parent's bedroom on the small platform rocker that had once belonged to Aunt Claribel. Were his tears triggered by his memory of that tragic day? Was he still struggling with his own uncertainty about the reason his father died by suicide?

I occasionally cried, too, especially after stressful days when I had few answers for the parents of seriously ill children. Each time, I thought of my dad and grieved for his loss. I especially grieved for his inability to share the lives and accomplishments of his own children, my brother and me, with his father. As I have learned from my own experiences, grandparents and their grandchildren have unique and cherished relationships. My grandfather's suicide took them all away.

I've often wondered what my grandfather saw and felt in his last moments. Did my grandfather see any of the good things, like the remarkable races he won or the pleasant days at The Maples, or did he only feel pain and sadness for his perceived failures? What were his final thoughts as he placed the shotgun against his head and pulled the trigger? Like some people who attempt suicide and survive, did his thoughts include a sudden regret for his action?

And what did my father see just before he died of heart failure in July 1997? Did he see his father? And if so, was it the disfigured man in the corn crib or the one who had carried him lovingly as they walked the fields and found arrowheads together? Although my dad could never erase the painful memory of that tragic day, he had always tried to do the next best thing. He used the memory, I believe, as motivation to do everything he could for our family, his schools, and the community.

I close with my thoughts about suicide intervention. I hesitate to say prevention because not all suicides can be prevented, despite our best efforts. But some can be prevented, and we must never lose sight of this goal. First and foremost, we must take people seriously when they say that they're considering suicide. We must listen, and we must ask questions.

We should begin with open-ended questions, as much as possible, to allow people the opportunity to express their feelings and concerns. "Tell me about it" is a simple and effective way to start the conversation. Then, we must be direct and specific in our questioning. Have they been thinking about hurting themselves? Have they wished that they were not alive? Do they believe that the world would be better off without them? Do they have a plan to end their lives? Have they ever acted on this plan?

Although we once worried that asking difficult questions could provoke people to attempt suicide, all recent studies suggest that we will not harm people by asking them about suicide. My mother's innate stubbornness led her to deflect my probing questions, but her empathy as a nurse prevented her from asking my dad about his father's death. She saw my father's tears, too, and these only reinforced her silence. My mom's fear of asking about suicide, perhaps the result of her nursing education in the 1940s, was a major reason, I believe, that she avoided the conversation.

Above all, we must remind people who are considering suicide that they are valued, loved, and needed by those around them. Suicide is frequently an impulsive act, and reminders of our love can be life-saving. Could we have prevented my Iowa colleague's suicide with occasional words of praise and simple acts of kindness?

We must remain alert for the warning signs of suicide. According to the National Institutes of Mental Health, the signs that someone may be at immediate risk of attempting suicide include:

- Talking about wanting to die or wanting to kill themselves
- Talking about feeling empty or hopeless or having no reason to live
- Talking about feeling trapped or feeling that there are no solutions

- Feeling unbearable emotional or physical pain
- Talking about being a burden to others
- Withdrawing from family and friends
- Giving away important possessions
- Saying goodbye to friends and family
- Putting affairs in order, such as making a will
- Taking great risks that could lead to death, such as driving extremely fast
- Talking or thinking about death often

Source: (https://www.nimh.nih.gov/health/topics/suicide-prevention)

I believe that my grandfather may have displayed some of these signs, even as a young man, but his family (*my* family) and friends likely had a limited understanding of their significance. The Michigan State Police report of that fateful day in 1943 suggests that while my relatives sensed that something was wrong with my grandfather, they didn't know what it was or what they could or should do. Decades would pass before our understanding of suicide risk factors and warning signs would enable intervention and prevention.

Finally, we must ask despondent people about their firearms, and we *must* offer to keep their guns safe while they work through their emotions. More than one-half of all suicides in America result from firearm use, especially among men. With its 400 million guns—more than one firearm for every man, woman, and child—the U.S. has unacceptably high rates of gun violence, including suicide. While we may never succeed in removing all weapons, we can remove them selectively and protect the lives of the most vulnerable people in the process. If only a loaded shotgun had not been in the barn.

A corn crib on the Bale farm similar to the one in which my
grandfather shot himself

Source: The author

Epilogue

I'm certain now that the stigma of suicide led my family to create the story of the hawk and lie to me when I was young. Over the years, I told the story of my grandfather's accident to numerous friends and their families, and virtually everyone who heard it expressed their sympathy. I wonder. Would they have reacted differently if I had told them that my grandfather died by suicide? Did my childhood friends actually like me better because of the lie?

I've also wondered about how an earlier knowledge of my grandfather's suicide might have influenced my interactions with others. Would I have been more sensitive to the needs and feelings of my friends when I was young and less egocentric as an adolescent? Would I have been humbler and more empathetic? Or could it have had the opposite effect?

As a teenager, one chaotic Christmas, I shouted to my parents, "At least I'm not going to commit suicide!" I don't remember what provoked my outburst, but I do remember that my mother gasped audibly when I uttered those words. At the time, I thought that her reaction was intended for me and never suspected that her concern was for my father, who sat nearby, quietly listening to my tirade. Would I have responded differently to teenage stress had I known about my grandfather's suicide?

And if there is a genetic susceptibility to suicide, could the knowledge of his suicide have been an additional factor that increased my own risk of attempting suicide as a teenager? Could knowing the truth have been a tragic tipping point?

So, maybe my mother's decision to avoid the truth until I reached adulthood was the correct one after all. On balance, it now seems that the knowledge of the real story could have been more detrimental to me as a child than beneficial. Just like she carefully managed our family's financial health, did my mom intentionally withhold the information about my grandfather's death until she felt confident that I had the emotional maturity to process it?

Because my family chose to hide the truth, I lack answers to my questions. Frankly, that always seems to be the case. The survivors of suicide, and I consider myself one, are left with many more questions than answers.

The Bale Family Tree

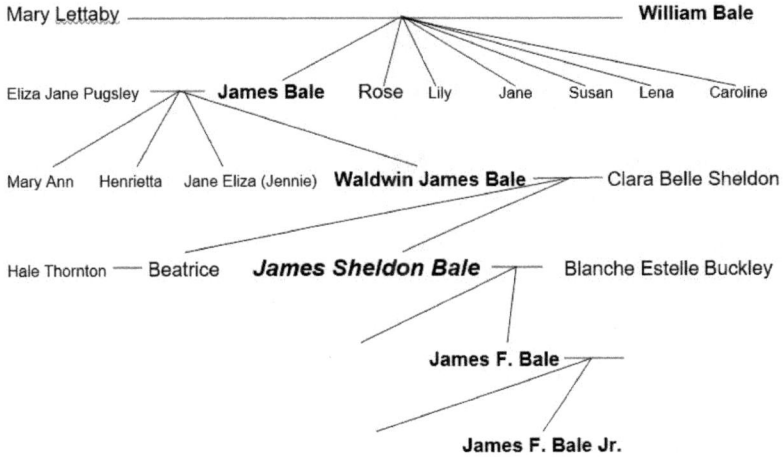

Mary Lettaby ——————————————————————— **William Bale**

Eliza Jane Pugsley ——— **James Bale**   Rose   Lily   Jane   Susan   Lena   Caroline

Mary Ann   Henrietta   Jane Eliza (Jennie)   **Waldwin James Bale** ——— Clara Belle Sheldon

Hale Thornton —— Beatrice   *James Sheldon Bale* ——— Blanche Estelle Buckley

James F. Bale ———

James F. Bale Jr.

Photographs and Illustrations

Chapter 1: Ilfracombe

Bale ancestors.
Vintage stereograph of Ilfracombe's harbor, date unknown.
Hele Bay and Beach, circa 1840.
Ilfracombe cliffs sketched by James Bale, circa 1840.

Chapter 2: Ships Passing in the Night

Fitz Henry Lane (1804-1865), Unicorn, Salem Harbor, 1840.
Albert dock, Liverpool, England, present day.
Rose Bale, Grandpa Bale's sister, date unknown.

Chapter 3: Paw Paw

Grandpa Bale, date unknown.
Gravestone of Eaven Bale, first son of James and Eliza Bale.
Paw Paw's Methodist Episcopal church, circa 1915.
Patent diagram. J. Bale and A. E. Lapham, 1898.
Stephentown, NY. Founded by Clara Belle Sheldon's ancestors.

Chapter 4: The Maples: Part 1

West-facing master bedroom window.
The Bale farmhouse viewed from the east in the early 1900s.

Gingerbread and decorative fretwork above a second floor window.
A Boot Island cottage designed and built by Grandpa Bale.
Grandpa Bale's tool chest, exterior.
Some of Grandpa Bale's hand tools.
A storage shed, likely used as the ice house.
The 'House on Fire' granary in Mule Canyon, Southeast Utah.
The Bale farmhouse, showing architectural embellishments.

Chapter 5: The Maples: Part 2

Hickory trees northwest of the Bale farmhouse.
Woodlot south of Red Arrow highway.
Shed or cabin that might have housed migrant farm laborers.
One end of a Welch's wood grape lug.
Vineyard near Lawton, Michigan.
Early advertisement for Paw Paw grape juice.

Chapter 6: Another James Bale

Some of the arrowheads and points found on the farm.
My father, James Bale, age 17.
Bendix Male Chorus. Dad is third from the left, front row.
Superintendent of Schools, James F. Bale, at his desk in Three Oaks.

Chapter 7: Mom, I-94, and the Great Recession

Interstate highway bridge over the Mississippi River, present day.
Marilyn, my mom, age 3 years.
One of grandfather's eye cups.
Grandfather at Pilgrim Manor, Grand Rapids, Michigan.
My mom, circa 1950s.
Stockholm, Sweden, 2019.

Chapter 8: Taylor the Tailor

Chapter 9: The Underground Railroad

Chapter 10: The Truth

Chapter 11: Suicide

Epilogue

Cover

Suicide Resources

1. 988 Suicide and Crisis Lifeline. Dial or Text 988. The Lifeline provides support 24/7.

2. Crisis Text Line. Text HOME to 741741 to connect with a volunteer Crisis Counselor.

3. National Alliance for Mental Illness. NAMI. Call the NAMI Helpline at 1-800-950-6264 or text "Helpline" to 62640.

4. U. S. Substance Abuse and Mental Health Services Administration (SAMHSA). https://www.samhsa.gov/find-help

5. National Institutes of Mental Health. Suicide Prevention. https://www.nimh.nih.gov/health/topics/suicide-prevention

6. American Foundation for Suicide Prevention (AFSP). 1-888-333-AFSP (2377). https://afsp.org/about-afsp/

7. Center for Disease Control and Prevention. Suicide Prevention: Prevention Strategies. https://www.cdc.gov/suicide/prevention/index.html

8. American Psychiatric Association. Suicide Prevention. https://www.psychiatry.org/patients-families/suicide-prevention

9. Mental Health Foundation-UK. https://www.mentalhealth.org.uk/

10. Government of Canada. Public Health Agency of Canada. Suicide Prevention. https://www.canada.ca/en/public-health/services/suicide-prevention.html

11. Pan American Health Organization Suicide Prevention. https://www.paho.org/en/topics/suicide-prevention

12, Minnesota Department of Agriculture: Coping with Farm and Rural Stress. https://www.mda.state.mn.us/about/mnfarmerstress

Sources and Additional Readings

All links accessed successfully on August 6, 2024.

Chapter 1: Ilfracombe.

- British Literature WIKI. Education in Victorian England. https://sites.udel.edu/britlitwiki/education-in-victorian-england/
- Geison, G. The Private Science of Louis Pasteur. Princeton University Press. 1995.
- GenUKI. https://www.genuki.org.uk/
- Germ theory. https://curiosity.lib.harvard.edu/contagion/feature/germ-theory
- Higham, T. The World before us. The New Science behind our Human Origins. Yale University Press. New Haven. 2021. p. 220.
- Holy Trinity Church, Ilfracombe. https://en.wikipedia.org/wiki/Holy_Trinity_Church,_Ilfracombe
- Humoral theory. https://curiosity.lib.harvard.edu/contagion/feature/humoral-theory
- Ilfracombe. White's Devonshire Directory of 1850. https://www.genuki.org.uk/big/eng/DEV/Ilfracombe/Ilfracombe1850
- Johnston, M. Victorian Trades: the carpenter, house joiner and cabinet maker. March 27, 2021. https://www.historic-design.com/victorian-trades-the-carpenter-house-joiner-and-cabinet-maker/
- Jones, C. Diseases that wouldn't die: Why are so many Victorian

killer illnesses making a comeback? Nov. 2012. https://www.mirror.co.uk/news/real-life-stories/victorian-killer-diseases-like-rickets-1432819

- Koch's postulates. https://www.sciencedirect.com/topics/medicine-and-dentistry/kochs-postulates
- Michael and Maddison. Education in England during the 1800s. https://prezi.com/gvj4zyu4_n34/education-in-england-during-the-1800s/
- Sakai, T., Morimoto, Y. The history of infectious diseases and medicine. Pathogens 11:1147, 2022.
- The Geology of South West England. https://earthwise.bgs.ac.uk/index.php/South-west_England_area_-_Geology#:~:text
- Toledo-Pereyra, L. H. A critical study of Lister's work on antiseptic surgery. Am J Surg 131:736-44, 1976.
- University of Leeds. Leeds General Cemetery. Ten ways to die in Victorian England. https://livingwithdying.leeds.ac.uk/2017/08/09/top-ten-ways-to-die-in-victorian-britain/

Chapter 2: Ships Passing in the Night.

- Buildings at Risk. Scott's Dry Dock. https://www.buildingsatrisk.org.uk/details/910213
- Family Search. Free Online New York Passenger Lists, 1820-1897. M237. Roll 79. p. 544. https://www.familysearch.org/en/wiki/Free_Online_New_York_Passenger_Lists,_1820-1897
- Kipling, R. The Burning of the Sarah Sands. The Kipling Society. https://www.kiplingsociety.co.uk/tale/the-burning-of-the-sarah-sands.htm
- Mary Seacole. The Wonderful Adventures of Mrs. Seacole in Many Lands. https://www.history.co.uk/article/the-wonderful-adventures-of-mrs-seacole-in-many-lands
- Rappaport, H. No Place for Ladies. The Untold Story of Women in the Crimean War. Aurum Press. 2007.

- Schlotel, F. Burning of the Sarah Sands. Bemrose and Sons. London. 1870.
- Scottish Built Ships. The Unicorn. https://www.clyde-ships.co.uk/view.phpofficial_number=&imo=&builder=&builder_eng=&year_built=&launch_after=&launch_before=&role=&type_ref1=&propulsion=&owner=&port=&flag=&disposal=&lost=&ref=21843&vessel=UNICORN
- Selanders, L. Florence Nightingale: British nurse, statistician, and social reformer. In: Encyclopedia Britannica. https://www.britannica.com/biography/Florence-Nightingale

Chapter 3: Paw Paw.

- History of Paw Paw Township, Michigan. Parts 1 to 3. From: History of Berrien and Van Buren Counties, Michigan. D. W. Ensign & Co. J. B. Lippincott & Co. Philadelphia, PA. 1880.
- History.com. Walter Raleigh. https://www.history.com/topics/exploration/walter-raleigh
- Kalamazoo Gazette. Methodist Church in Paw Paw Replica of Old English Place of Worship. Sunday, November 30, 1941. page 3-section two.
- Kemkes, A. Smothered infants-neglect, infanticide or SIDS? A fresh look at the 19th century mortality schedules. Human Ecology 37:393-405, 2009.
- Teelander, A. 1st Michigan Engineers and Mechanics Roster. Images of Michigan. https://www.migenweb.org/michiganinthe-war/engineers/1enga.htm
- Van Buren County Historical Society. History of Van Buren County, Michigan. 1982. Taylor Publishing Co. Dallas, Tx. 1983. pp. 41-2.
- Village of Paw Paw Michigan. https://www.pawpaw.net/about

Chapter 4: The Maples, Part 1.

- Red Arrow Highway. Barnett, LeRoy. A Drive Down Memory Lane: The Named State and Federal Highways of Michigan. Allegan Forest, MI: The Priscilla Press. 2004.
- Garraty, J. A. The Great Depression. Harcourt, Brace, Jovanovich Publishers. San Diego, CA. 1986.
- Granary. https://en.wikipedia.org/wiki/Granary
- Silage. https://en.wikipedia.org/wiki/Silage#:~:text=Silage
- Silo. https://en.wikipedia.org/wiki/Silo
- Skjelver, M. C. Nineteenth Century Homes of Marshall, Michigan. Marshall Historical Society. Marshall, Michigan. 1971.

Chapter 5: The Maples, Part 2.

- Boyle, T. C. The Road to Wellville. Viking Press. New York. 1993.
- Chazanof, W. Welch's Grape Juice: From Corporation to Co-operative. Syracuse. Syracuse University Press. 1977.
- Dean, S. History of the PB&J, from spa food to school lunch. Bon Appétit. August 29, 2013.
- Freedman, J. E., Parker, C., 3rd, Li, L., et al. Select flavonoids and whole juice from purple grapes inhibit platelet function and enhance nitric oxide release. Circulation 103:2792-8, 2001.
- History of the Concord Grape. http://www.concordgrape.org/bodyhistory.html
- Kellogg, J. H. Home Handbook of Medicine and Hygiene. Revised edition. Modern Medicine Publishing Co. Battle Creek, MI. 1896. p. 1010.
- National Peanut Butter Board. http:/www.nationalpeanut-board.org/news/who-invented-the-peanut-butter-and-jelly-sandwich.htm
- Pollan, M. The Botany of Desire: A Plant's Eye View of the World. Random House. 2001.
- Puchko, K. 9 Facts that tell the true story of Johnny Appleseed.

Sep 26, 2017. http://mentalfloss.com/article/62113/9-facts-tell-true-story-johnny-appleseed

- Rupp, R. The highs and lows of hard cider history. National Geographic. October 8, 2015.
- Smith, A. Food and Drink in American History. Volume 1: A-L. ABC-CLIO. Santa Barbara, CA. 2013.
- Zeratsky, K. Does grape juice offer the same heart benefits as red wine. https://www.mayoclinic.org/healthy-lifestyle/nutrition-and-healthy-eating/expert-answers/food-and-nutrition/faq-20058529

Chapter 6: Another James Bale.

- Clark Equipment https://www.clarkmhc.com/Company/History
- Mason, P. P. Early Indian Trails Traced Highways of the Future from Footpaths to Expressway. Chicago Road. 1958.
- Mason, P. P. Michigan Highways: From Indian Trails to Expressways. Michigan Historical Commission. Detroit, MI. October 1959.
- Michiana Male Chorus. https://www.michianamalechorus.org/
- Peter Gent. https://en.wikipedia.org/wiki/Peter_Gent\
- St. Joseph Herald Press. Bendix male chorus. October 12, 1945. p. 3.

Chapter 7: Mom, I-94, and the Great Recession.

- Benton Harbor demographics. https://www.neighborhood-scout.com/mi/benton-harbor/demographics
- Boeing B17 Flying Fortress. http://www.aviation-history.com/boeing/b17.html
- Consolidated B24 Liberator. http://www.aviation-history.com/consolidated/b24.html
- Davis, D. Is Battle Creek still the 'Cereal City'? It's complicated, officials say. Battle Creek Inquirer. June 12, 2017.

- Forbes, M. K. Krueger, R. K. The great recession and mental health in the United States. Clin Psychol Sci 7:900-13, 2019.
- History of I-94 in Michigan. https://en.wikipedia.org/wiki/Interstate_94_in_Michigan
- History of the Interstate Highway System. https://en.wikipedia.org/wiki/Interstate_Highway_System
- Kalamazoo College. https://en.wikipedia.org/wiki/Kalamazoo_College
- Kerr, W. C., Kaplan, M. S., et al. Economic recession, alcohol, and suicide rates: Comparative effects of poverty, foreclosure, and job loss. Am J Prev Med 52:469–75, 2017.
- Michigan Department of Treasury: Office of Revenue and Tax Analysis. Michigan Economic Update. September 2009 Summary.
  https://www.michigan.gov/documents/treasury/MEU-September09_300287_7.pdf
- Pope, L. Colleges that Change Lives. Penguin Books. 2013.
- Reeves, A., McKee, M., Stuckler, D. Economic suicides in the Great Recession in Europe and North America. Br J Psychiatry 205:246-7, 2014.
- Rosie the Riveter. https://www.history.com/topics/world-war-ii/rosie-the-riveter
- St. Joseph demographics. https://www.neighborhoodscout.com/mi/st-joseph/demographics
- Unemployment rates by State. December 2023. https://www.bls.gov/web/laus/laumstrk.htm
- U. S. Department of Labor. Careeronestop. Michigan State Profile. Largest Employers. https://www.careerinfonet.org/oview6.asp?soccode=&stfips=26&from=State&id=11&nodeid=12
- Watkins, T. H. The Great Depression. Little, Brown and Company. Boston. 1993.
- Willow Run Expressway. Ann Arbor News. July 15, 1972. p. 12.
- Wyatt, K. Peek Through Time: A look back at Jackson County

settlers' relationships with Indians https://www.mlive.com/news/jackson/2011/06/peek_through_time_a_look_back.html

Chapter 8: Taylor the Tailor,

- Catton, B. Michigan. A History. W. W. Norton and Company. New York. 1976.
- Hass, L. Hidden in Plain Sight. The Underground Railroad in Jackson County. BookLocker, Inc. 1st edition. 2008. pp. 15-22.
- Kolchin, P. American Slavery. 1619 – 1877. Hill and Wang. New York. 2003.
- Morehouse, L. Taylor the Tailor, Jackson, Michigan.
- Passenger Ships - 19th Century. https://www.globalsecurity.org/military/systems/ship/passenger-19.htm
- Passenger Ships – 19th Century. Children of the ocean. http://norwayheritage.com/children.htm
- Peyrol-Kleiber, E. Starting Afresh: Freedom dues vs reality in 17th century Chesapeake. https://doi.org/10.4000/mimmoc.2777
- Solem, B. Steerage. http://www.norwayheritage.com/steerage.htm
- Suranyi, A. Indentured servitude in Colonial America. https://doi.org/10.1093/acrefore/9780199329175.013.1125
- Township of Spring Arbor, Michigan. History. https://springarbor.org/about/history/
- United States. Bureau of Customs. National Archives and Records Service. Passenger lists of vessels arriving at New York, 1820 – 1897. Reel 0017, p. 227. https://archive.org/details/passengerlistsof0017unix/page/n227/mode/2up
- United States Department of Labor. Bureau of Labor Statistics. History of wages in the United States from Colonial times to 1928. United States Government Printing Office. Washington, D. C. 1929.
- Wolfe, B. Slave Ships. Encyclopedia Virginia. https://encyclopediavirginia.org/entries/slave-ships-and-the-middle-passage/

Chapter 9: The Underground Railroad.

- American History Central. The Headright System in Colonial America. https://www.americanhistorycentral.com/entries/headright-system-in-colonial-america/#:~:text
- Anglican church apologizes for its role in slavery. https://historynewsnetwork.org/article/21566
- Charleston, South Carolina. https://en.wikipedia.org/wiki/Charleston,_South_Carolina
- Constitution of the United States. https://en.wikipedia.org/wiki/Constitution_of_the_United_States
- Free-Will Baptists and Slavery. https://fwbhistory.com/?p=467
- Fugitive Slave Acts. https://www.history.com/topics/black-history/fugitive-slave-acts
- History of Slavery in New York. https://en.wikipedia.org/wiki/History_of_slavery_in_New_York_(state)
- Kneeland, L. K. Master of Arts Thesis. African American Suffering and Suicide Under Slavery. Montana State University. 2006. https://scholarworks.montana.edu/xmlui/handle/1/1654
- Macclesfield Sunday School. https://en.wikipedia.org/wiki/Macclesfield_Sunday_School
- Methodist Church History. https://www.learnreligions.com/methodist-church-history-700976
- Slavery. https://en.wikipedia.org/wiki/Slavery
- The Constitution of the United States – a transcription. https://www.archives.gov/founding-docs/constitution-transcript
- The Holy Bible. King James version. Exodus, chapter 5, verse 1.
- Underground Railroad. https://education.nationalgeographic.org/resource/underground-railroad

Chapter 10: The Truth.

- Egan, T. The Worst Hard Time. Houghton Mifflin Company. 2006.
- Fatal shooting is probed by police. South Haven Daily Tribune. September 23, 1943. https://newspaperarchive.com/south-haven-daily-tribune-sep-21-1943-p-1/

Chapter 11: Suicide.

- Ashley-Koch, A., Kimbrel, N., Qin, X., et al. Genome-wide association study identifies four pan-ancestry loci for suicidal ideation in the Million Veteran Program. PLoS Genet 19: e1010623, 2023.
- Baumeister, R. https://en.wikipedia.org/wiki/Roy_Baumeister
- Centers for Disease Control and Prevention. Suicide rates by industry and occupation — National Violent Death Reporting System, 32 States, 2016. https://www.cdc.gov/mmwr/volumes/69/wr/mm6903a1.htm
- DiBlasi, E., Kang, J., Docherty, A. Genetic contributions to suicidal thoughts and behaviors. Psychological Medicine 51:2148–2155, 2021.
- Docherty, A., Mullins, N., Ashley-Koch, A., et al. GWAS Meta-Analysis of Suicide Attempt: Identification of 12 Genome-Wide Significant Loci and Implication of Genetic Risks for Specific Health Factors. Am J Psychiatry 180: 723–738, 2023.
- Four dead in rampage in an Iowa Town. https://www.ny-times.com/1985/12/10/us/4-dead-in-rampage-in-an-iowa-town.html
- Gerstel, J. Why middle-aged men are at high risk for suicide. https://www.everythingzoomer.com/health/2020/09/10/suicide-middle-age-recognize-signs/
- Hartman, C. On the road: Johnson County, Iowa. https://www.inc.com/magazine/19860501/839.html

- Iowa College of Public Health. Research: Farmers still take their own lives at high rates. June 13, 2017. https://www.public-health.uiowa.edu/news-items/research-farmers-still-take-own-lives-at-a-high-rate/
- Kimbrel, N., Garrett, M., Evans, M., et al. Large epigenome-wide association study identifies multiple novel differentially methylated CpG sites associated with suicidal thoughts and behaviors in veterans. Front Psychiatry 14:1145375, 2023.
- Mayo Clinic Staff. Suicide grief. https://www.mayoclinic.org/healthy-lifestyle/end-of-life/in-depth/suicide/art-20044900
- Minnesota Department of Agriculture. Business, financial and legal help. https://www.mda.state.mn.us/about/mnfarmerstress/busfinlegalhelp
- Mirza, S., Docherty, A., Bakian, A., et al. Genetics and epigenetics of self-injurious thoughts and behaviors: Systematic review of the suicide literature and methodological considerations. Am J Med Genet B Neuropsychiatr Genet 189: 221–246, 2022.
- Mullins, N., Kang, JE., Campos, A., et al. Dissecting the shared genetic architecture of suicide attempt: Psychiatric disorders, and known risk factors. Biol Psychiatry 91:313-327, 2022.
- National Institutes of Mental Health. What are the warning signs of suicide? https://www.nimh.nih.gov/health/topics/suicide-prevention
- Nelson, K. All I wanted to do was live. CNN. November 23, 2023. https://www.ksl.com/article/50794381/all-i-wanted-to-do-was-live-suicide-safety-net-for-golden-gate-bridge-nears-completion
- Olson, R. Why do people kill themselves? https://www.suicide-info.ca/local_resource/suicidetheories/
- Plumpte, E. Self-deprecation: Harmless habit or unhealthy behavior. https://www.verywellmind.com/what-is-self-deprecation-5186918
- Ringgenberg, W., Peek-Asa, C., et al. Trends and characteristics

of occupational suicide and homicide in farmers and agriculture workers, 1992-2010. J Rural Health 34:246-253, 2018.

- Suicide Notes. https://www.psychologytoday.com/us/blog/shadow-boxing/201210/suicide-notes
- Tyrell, P., Harberger, S., Schoo, C., Siddiqui, W. Kubler-Ross states of dying and subsequent models of grief. In: StatPearls [Internet]. Treasure Island (FL): StatPearls Publishing; 2024.

Printed in the USA
CPSIA information can be obtained
at www.ICGtesting.com
LVHW022220280924
792287LV00001B/1

9 798218 421434